HISTORY OF ISLAM

Umayyad & Abbasid Khilaafat, Islamic empires, Imaams of fiqh And recent history

Published By : Islamic Book Store

Title: **History of Islam**
(Umayyad & Abbasid Khilaafat,
Islamic empires, Imaams of fiqh
And recent history)

Prepared by:
Jamiatul Ulama (KZN)
Ta'limi Board
4 Third Avenue
P.O.Box 26024
Isipingo Beach
4115
South Africa

Tel: (+27) 31 912 2172
Fax: (+27) 31 902 9268
E-mail: info@talimiboardkzn.org
Website: www.talimiboardkzn.org

First edition: January 2018 / 1438

Published by:
Islamic Book Store
302 Saad Residancy
Sahin Park M G Road
Bardoli Surat Gujarat
India 394601
UDYAM REGISTRATION NUMBER :
UDYAM-GJ-22-0457400

Contents

Introduction I
Notes to the Teacher III
    General Guidelines for Teachers IV
    General Guidelines, outlining this book V

PART ONE 2

Theory of Evolution 2
Ambiyaa عَلَيْهِمُ ٱلسَّلَام 4
Khulafaa - e - Raashideen 6
A Brief history of Shiasm 8
Hadhrat Hasan رَضِيَ ٱللَّهُ عَنْهُ 16
    Appointment as Khalifah 16
    Peace treaty with Hadhrat Mu'aawiyah رَضِيَ ٱللَّهُ عَنْهُ 20
    Death 20
The Umayyad Khilaafat – 95 Years 21
    Achivements of the Banu Umayya 23
Hadhrat Mu'aawiyah رَضِيَ ٱللَّهُ عَنْهُ 25
    Expedition to Constantinople (Istanbul) 27
    Summary of the Achievements of Hadhrat Mu'aawiyah's رَضِيَ ٱللَّهُ عَنْهُ Khilaafat 28
    The succession of Hadhrat Mu'aawiyah رَضِيَ ٱللَّهُ عَنْهُ 29
    Death of Hadhrat Mu'aawiyah (radhiyallahu anhu) 30
Hadhrat Abdullah bin Zubair رَضِيَ ٱللَّهُ عَنْهُ 31
    Martydom of Hadhrat Abdullah bin Zubair (radhiyallahu anhu) 33
Yazeed bin Mu'aawiyah 35
    Appointment to Khilaafat 35
    Events leading to the Battle of Karbala 36
    The Battle of Karbala 42
    Yazeed's Successor 44
Abdul Malik bin Marwaan 73 to 86 A.H. (13 Years) 45
Waleed bin Abdul Malik 86 to 96 A.H. (10 Years) 45
Umar bin Abdul Aziz رَحِمَهُ ٱللَّهُ 99 to 101 A.H. (2 Years) 46

    Appointment as governor and Khalifah..................................... 47
    Simplicity and popularity 48
    Death 49
MUHAMMAD BIN QAASIM **50**
CONQUEST OF SPAIN - 92 A.H. **52**

PART TWO 54

THE ABBASID KHILAAFAT... **54**
EXTENT OF THE ABBASID EMPIRE **56**
ABUL ABBAAS AS SAFFAH **57**
MANSUR **57**
HAROON AR-RASHEED **59**
MUHAMMAD AL-AMEEN BIN HAROON **60**
MA'MUN AR-RASHEED... **61**
DECLINE OF THE ABBASID KHILAAFAT **62**
ACHIEVEMENTS OF THE ABBASID KHILAAFAT....................................... **63**
THE CRUSADES... **64**
SALAHUDDIN AYYUBI **66**
MUSLIM EMPIRES BETWEEN THE 14TH AND 19TH CENTURY...................... **68**
THE OTTOMAN EMPIRE - 1200 TO 1924 C.E. **70**
    The Arabian front: 73
    The Palestinian front: 74
THE MONGOLS 1206 C.E. - 1370 C.E. (164 YEARS)......................... **77**
GENGHIS (CHANGHEZ) KHAN (1206 - 1227 C.E.) **77**
HULAGU KHAN.. **77**
THE MONGOLS ACCEPT ISLAM **79**
MAP SHOWING THE EXTENT OF THE MOGUL EMPIRE **80**
THE MOGUL EMPIRE OF INDIA 1526 TO 1857 C.E. **81**
BABUR **81**
HUMAYUN **82**
AKBAR **82**
JAHANGIR **84**
SHAH JAHAN **86**
AURANGZEB (AALAMGEER) **87**
THE FALL OF THE MOGUL EMPIRE **89**

PART THREE 92

THE IMPORTANCE OF TAQLEED AND A BRIEF HISTORY OF THE FOUR IMAAMS 92
Submitting oneself to the commands of Allah Ta'ala as shown to mankind by Ambiyaa (alayhimus salaam); 92
Definition and the importance of Taqleed; 93
Why follow one Imaam only? 95

BRIEF LIFE SKETCHES OF THE FOUR IMAAMS FROM WHOM THE FOUR MAZHABS ORIGINATED 97
IMAAM ABU HANIFA رَحِمَهُ ٱللَّهُ 97
IMAAM MAALIK رَحِمَهُ ٱللَّهُ 100
IMAAM SHAFI'EE رَحِمَهُ ٱللَّهُ 101
IMAAM AHMAD BIN HAMBAL رَحِمَهُ ٱللَّهُ 102
MAP OF PALESTINE 103
PALESTINE 104
Population 104
Islam in Palestine, the UN mandate and recent events 104
Why Palestine is important to the Muslims? 109

ISLAM IN SOUTH AFRICA 111
SHAIKH YUSUF 111
THE RAJAH OF TAMBORA (ABDUL BASI SULTANA) 112
DE VRYEZWARTEN 112
TUANG GURU (ABDULLAH BIN QADHI ABDUS SALAAM) 113
THE ARRIVAL OF MUSLIMS OF INDIAN ORIGIN 114
MUSLIMS FROM ZANZIBAR 116
ISLAMIC ORGANISATIONS IN SOUTH AFRICA 116

Map showing extent of Arabia, Parts of Africa, the Persian and roman Empires and Shaam (Syria), which was part of the Roman Empire

Introduction

Rasulullah ﷺ has said, **"Hold onto my Sunnah and the Sunnah of my Righteous Khulafaa after me."** The Sahaabah-e-Kiraam (radhiyallahu anhum) were beacons of guidance for the Ummah. Studying their lives, learning about them and following in their footsteps are indeed the recipe for the success of mankind.

Study of the different periods of Islamic history serves as lessons to us and warns us to steer away from the downfalls of nations of the past and to wholeheartedly accept the rich legacy of the Ambiyaa (alayhimus salaam), the Khulafaa-e-Raashideen and all our pious predecessors who had followed them.

We see that when nations moved away from their true object (i.e. to establish the Deen of Allah Ta'ala) and engrossed themselves totally in worldly pursuits and advancements, then this became a cause of their downfall and paved the way for other nations to rule over them and subject them to tyranny and persecution.

In this book we will touch on the era which is after the Khulafaa-e-Raashideen period up to contemporary times. This is not a detail account of this period, but rather a skeletal outline giving the highlights so that we can get a broad perspective and understanding of our history after the Khulafaa-e-Raashideen

INTRODUCTION

period. History has always been one of the key tools for any nation reaching the peaks of success.

This subject, if taught correctly, can become the most enjoyable subject for any child. On the contrary, if it is just read out without properly explaining the events and the lessons behind each event, then it can also become the most boring and difficult subject for a learner. Teachers should try their best to be real, alive, and vivid when teaching this subject.

In the compilation of this book, reference was also made to the Tasheelut Taa-reekh of the Jamiatul Ulama Transvaal.

Ta'limi Board (KZN)
Safar 1439 (Nov 2017)

Notes to the Teacher

All praise is due to Allah Ta'ala. Durood and Salaam be upon our master Hadhrat Muhammad ﷺ. It is only with the Fadhal and grace of Allah Ta'ala that He has granted us an opportunity to teach Islamic history and the noble Seerah of His beloved Nabi ﷺ. If we can instil the true love of Nabi ﷺ, the Sahaabah (radhiyallahu anhum) and our pious predecessors into the hearts and minds of our young learners, we have achieved our greatest objective. If every learner in our class leaves with this feeling in his/her heart that Nabi ﷺ is my role model, then there is no greater achievement for us in this 21st century. May Allah Ta'ala bless us all with His true love and the love of His Nabi ﷺ, the Sahaabah (radhiyallahu anhum) and our pious predecessors and may He give us the ability to follow every sunnah of our beloved Nabi ﷺ.

Please take note of the following points when teaching Islamic history and the Seerah of Rasulullah ﷺ:

1. Make a chart with all the important dates and events and put it up on the wall in the classroom.
2. Before teaching a new lesson, explain the difficult terms and definitions e.g. Byzantine, Khilaafat, etc.

NOTES TO TEACHER

3. With the aid of maps, explain to the pupils the geographical location of the area being discussed.
4. After each lesson, have an oral question and answer session. This will give the teacher an indication as to what the Pupils have understood.

General Guidelines for Teachers

- Come well prepared for the lesson.
- Summarise the previous lesson before commencing a new lesson.
- Introduce the new lesson to the class by asking them general questions about the new lesson.
- Ensure that your lesson is properly time framed.
- Write down important / key words on the board.
- If you cannot take the children to Badr, bring Badr to the children. Also, show them maps so they can identify the relevant places being discussed.
- Do not just read the text out of a text book. Be active, full of life and expressive when teaching a lesson.
- Divorce your chair and marry the chalkboard.
- Summarise the lesson with quick oral questions.
- Make a written note of any weak area found in the lesson so that you can rectify it at a later stage.

NOTES TO TEACHER

General Guidelines, outlining this book

A brief summary of events from the beginning of time; from the time of creation of the earth to the period of the Khulafaa-e-Raashideen **(A to D below)** was covered from grade 1 to grade 7. This book will, Insha-Allah, cover the period after the Khulafaa-e-Raashideen up to contemporary times **(E to G below)**. A brief recap of the points listed below must be done with the pupils so that they can identify which period in history is being taught to them. The pupils must be explained points A to C below in brief so that they can identify where exactly The Umayyad Khilaafat, The Abaasad Khilaafat, etc. fit in.

PART ONE

A. Creation of the earth by Allah Ta'ala (not by the big bang theory and **evolution**).
B. Coming of the **Ambiyaa (alayhimus salaam)** from Hadhrat Aadam (alayhis salaam) to Hadhrat Isa (alayhis salaam) and the finality of Nubuwat by the last Nabi, Hadhrat Muhammad ﷺ.
C. The four **Khulafaa-e-Raashideen**, Hadhrat Abu Bakr, Hadhrat Umar, Hadhrat Uthmaan and Hadhrat Ali (radhiyallahu anhum).
D. A brief history of **Shiasm**.

NOTES TO TEACHER

E. The **Umayyad Khilaafat, Muhammad bin Qaasim & Spain**.

PART TWO

F. The **Abbaasid Khilaafat**, The **crusades, Salahuddeen Ayyubi & Muslim Empires**.

PART THREE

G. The **four Imaams, Palestine & South African History**.

This book is recommended for pupils in **Grades eight to twelve**. For revision purposes, pupils should be encouraged to read the following books of Islamic History;

1. "Basic History" on Ambiyaa (alayhimus salaam).
2. "Seerah of Muhammad ﷺ".
3. "Seeratul Mustafa ﷺ" Abridged.
4. "Khulafaa-e-Raashideen" Grade seven.

KEY WORDS

To really appreciate and comprehend any book, the teacher should ensure that the pupil understands key words that will make the subject at hand easier to digest and more enjoyable. Hereunder is a list of words contained in this book. Try to understand these words and abbreviations before starting this book.

A.H.	Denotes the year After Hijrat
C.E.	Christian Era (The year according to the Gregorian date)
Allied forces	Refers to the USA, Britain, France & other western nations
Ambiyaa	Plural of Nabi
Balkans	Eastern Europe; Greece, Romania, Serbia, Croatia, etc.
Byzantine	Eastern Roman Empire with Constantinople (Istanbul) as capital
Caucasus	Includes Georgia, Azerbaijan & South West Russia
Colonial	Rule and laws of a conquering nation imposed on a conquered nation
Constantinople	Present day Istanbul in Turkey
Dinar	Gold coin

KEY WORDS

Dynasty	A succession of people from the same family in power
Empire	Group of countries led by one single leader
Governor	Head of a particular province or state in an empire
Jazira	Upper Mesopotamia
Khilaafat	The responsibility of the position of the Khalifh
Khulafaa-e-Rashideen	The rightly guided Khalifhs
Mandate	One body empowers an authority to administer and govern and affairs of another nation
Mesopotamia	Land between the Tigris and Euphrates rivers in Iraq
Moguls	The ruling dynasty in India 1526-1827
Mongols	A tribe from east central Asia (Mongolia)
Nubia	North Sudan and South Egypt
Protectorate	A weak country governed or given protection by a strong country to a certain extent
Succeed	To take over position of authority
Tahneek	The practice of chewing a date and placing a portion of it in the mouth of a child to allow the saliva of Nabi ﷺ to link with the saliva of the child
Transoxia	Beyond the Oxus River - Central Asia, Uzbekistan, Tajikistan
Viceroy	Representative of the King in another town, province or country.

PART ONE

Theory of Evolution

We, the Muslims, deny the theory of evolution. This theory was made up by a person called Darwin. It is only speculation and has no truth in it. The fact that they call it a theory, suggests that it is not factual but only a theory. This theory explains that there is no divine being (i.e. our Creator Allah Ta'ala) and all life has come into existence after a huge explosion, 'The big bang' and thereafter evolved or changed through the ages.

This theory explains that man (insaan) was an ape or monkey and he has changed or evolved through thousands of years until he acquired his present physical appearance or form. To believe in this theory is kufr and takes a person out of the fold of Islam. Our belief is that the first man created by Allah Ta'ala was Aadam (alayhis salaam), and he was created in the most perfect form.

We are created by Allah Ta'ala in the most perfect form and our forefathers were not apes or monkeys. Regarding evolution we are sometimes influenced by our teachers in school, our professors in university and the text books that they use to teach us. We must be very clear of the fact that absolute truth is only in the words of Allah Ta'ala and His Rasul ﷺ. Allah Ta'ala had created

Aadam (alayhis salaam) in the most perfect form and the rest of humanity are the children of Aadam (alayhis salaam).

Lessons:

1. When taught any new theory or concept, which may be in conflict with our Deen, then always ask your Ustaaz, Ulama and pious seniors.
2. If you do not find out then your Imaan may be at risk.
3. In secular schools there are many things taught which are in direct conflict with the Sharia.
4. When in doubt, first find out.
5. Humans originated from Aadam (alayhis salaam) and not apes or monkeys.

Part One

Ambiyaa عَلَيْهِمُ ٱلسَّلَام

(The Messengers of Allah Ta'ala)

Allah Ta'ala had created this entire universe, including the sun, the planets, the stars, etc. to perfection and thereafter sent the first man, Aadam (alayhis salaam), to this earth and he was created in the most perfect form. Not only was he a human being, but Allah Ta'ala had also bestowed him with Nubuwat (Prophethood).

After Aadam (alayhis salaam), Allah Ta'ala sent down a chain of approximately one hundred and twenty four thousand Ambiyaa (alayhimus salaam) for the guidance of mankind. Some of these Ambiyaa (alayhimus salaam) include Ebrahim (alayhis salaam), Moosa (alayhis salaam), Isa (alayhis salaam), Dawood (alayhis salaam), Sulaiman (alayhis salaam), etc. This chain ended with the arrival of the last and final Nabi, Muhammadur Rasulullah صَلَّى ٱللَّهُ عَلَيْهِ وَسَلَّم. (Refer to "Basic History" for history on Ambiyaa (alayhimus salaam) and Grade 5 and 6 History for Seerah of Muhammad صَلَّى ٱللَّهُ عَلَيْهِ وَسَلَّم).

- 571 Years passed between the birth of **Rasulullah** صَلَّى ٱللَّهُ عَلَيْهِ وَسَلَّم and **Isa (alayhis salaam)**.
- 1716 Years passed between **Isa (alayhis salaam)** and **Moosa (alayhis salaam)**.

- 545 Years passed between **Moosa (alayhis salaam)** and **Ebrahim (alayhis salaam)**.
- 1081 Years passed between **Ebrahim (alayhis salaam)** and the flood of **Nuh (alayhis salaam)**.
- 2242 Years passed between the flood of **Nuh (alayhis salaam)** and **Aadam (alayhis salaam)**.
- According to this calculation, 6155 years passed between the birth of **Rasulullah** ﷺ and **Aadam (alayhis salaam)**.

Khulafaa - e - Raashideen

After the demise of Nabi Muhammad ﷺ came the period of the Khulafaa-e-Raashideen which started in 11 A.H. and lasted until 40 A.H. Islam was established in the Roman and the Persian empires and all these territories came under Muslim rule. The famous and decisive Battle of Yarmook brought the Roman Empire under Muslim rule and the Battle of Qaadisiyyah brought the Persian Empire under Muslim rule. (Refer to Grade 7 history book for history of the Khulafaa-e-Raashideen). The names of the pious righteous Khulafaa are as follows;

NO	IMAAMS	PLACE	PERIOD OF RULE
1	Abu Bakr رضي الله عنه	Madinah	11 to 13 A.H.
2	Umar رضي الله عنه	Madinah	13 to 24 A.H
3	Uthmaan رضي الله عنه	Madinah	24 to 35 A.H.
4	Ali رضي الله عنه	Kufa	35 to 40 A.H.
5	Hasan رضي الله عنه	Madinah	40 to 41 A.H.

Many historians say that the khilaafat of Hadhrat Hasan (radhiyallahu anhum) does not fall under the Khulafaa-e-Raashideen because of the very short period that he ruled. But if we take into account the manner in which he brought about peace, without shedding any blood and by handing over the khilaafat to Hadhrat Mu'aawiyah (radhiyallahu anhu), one will realise that this is in fact an important part of the Khilaafat-e-Raashidah.

Lessons:

1. If we claim we love Rasulullah ﷺ, then we must also show respect to his Sahaabah (radhiyallahu anhum).
2. No doubt Sahaabah (radhiyallahu anhum) had differences between them, but we have no right to comment or pass judgement on these noble companions of Rasulullah ﷺ.
3. We should always speak of the virtues of the Sahaabah (radhiyallahu anhum) and must guard our tongues against any negative comments about them.
4. Sit together with your family and read the "**Stories of Sahaabah**" (radhiyallahu anhum) from the Fazaail-e-Aamaal.
5. Any questions and doubts should be referred to your Ustaaz and **righteous Ulama**. They will always be glad to help you.
6. Rasulullah ﷺ said; "Observe silence in respect of my Sahaabah (when anything negative is mentioned or disrespect is shown to them)."
7. Allah Ta'ala declares in the Qur'aan that He is pleased with the Sahaabah (radhiyallahu anhum) and they are pleased with Him.

Part One

A Brief history of Shiasm

Origin of Shiasm

Long before the hijrat of Rasulullah ﷺ to Madinah Munawwarah, the Aus and the Khazraj tribes lived amongst the Jews in the city of Yathrib (Madinah Munawwarah). The Jews, who were from the Ahl-e-Kitaab, were much more knowledgeable than the Arabs, who were idol worshippers. The Jews enjoyed supremacy over the Arabs due to their knowledge and also financial muscle.

The Jews always kept the Aus and Khazraj tribes fighting each other by secretly carrying tales from one tribe to the other thus causing much bloodshed, loss of lives and damage and destruction to property. The Jews controlled Yathrib by using the age old weapon of "Divide and Rule", thereby subjugating the Arabs. The Arabs were also indebted to the Jews for the loans taken from the Jews. The Arabs had to pay exorbitant amounts of interest on the loans they had taken.

When Rasulullah ﷺ made hijrat to Madinah Munawwarah, he made peace between the Aus and Khazraj tribes and saved them from the clutches of the evil Jews. Being people of the book and knowledgeable in the scriptures, some Jews accepted Islam whilst many continued to live in kufr despite knowing deep down in their hearts that Rasulullah ﷺ was the true and last Prophet of Allah Ta'ala. The Jews could not swallow their pride and accept Rasulullah ﷺ as the last Prophet. The Jews continued with their evil plots and eventually joined forces with the kuffaar of Makkah to destroy the Muslims. Allah Ta'ala made them unsuccessful and they were eventually expelled from the Arabian Peninsula. Their hatred for Islam, Nabi Muhammad ﷺ and in particular the Sahaabah (radhiyallahu anhum) grew more and more every day. They tried belittling Nabi ﷺ and the Sahaabah (radhiyallahu anhum).

The Jews were now driven by rage and hopelessness. During the khilaafat of Hadhrat Uthmaan (radhiyallahu anhu) they found a leader who was a person well versed in treachery, lies, deception and sowing discord amongst people. His name was **Abdullah bin Sabah**. He joined the Muslim ranks disguised as a saint and won the hearts of many Muslims who were not familiar with the details of Islam. Taking advantage of their ignorance and seizing the opportunity to get back at the Muslims, Abdullah bin Sabah formulated his new religion, which later became known as **Shiasm**. His sole purpose was to destroy Islam from within as well as to establish himself as a political leader. This kaafir was the founder of Shiasm.

Part One

Abdullah bin Sabah, who was a good orator, influenced new reverts to Islam. He spoke out against the Qur-aan and the Sahaabah (radhiyallahu anhum) (the noble companions of Rasulullah ﷺ). He spoke very highly of Hadhrat Ali (radhiyallahu anhu) and elevated his status above the rest of the Sahaabah (radhiyallahu anhum) and in fact even more than Rasulullah ﷺ himself. He sometimes attributed divinity to Hadhrat Ali (radhiyallahu anhu) by claiming Ali (radhiyallahu anhu) to be Allah Ta'ala. The people who were weak in their imaan began to follow Abdullah bin Sabah. This was the beginning of the **false religion of Shiasm** which took root in many communities. Sadly, many Muslims believe that Shiasm is part of Islam and that there are no differences between the beliefs of the Ahlus Sunnah wal Jama'ah and the Shias. Shiasm is far from Islam. It is the only religion in the world that promotes lying, cheating, backbiting, adultery and all other sins as acts of worship.

After the assassination of Hadhrat Umar (radhiyallahu anhu), the Shias caused a lot of bloodshed and infighting in the Muslim Ummah. The murderer of Hadhrat Umar (radhiyallahu anhu), Abu Lulu the fire worshiper, had a mausoleum built around his grave by the Shias in Iran. The Shias revere this murderer because they hate Hadhrat Umar (radhiyallahu anhu), Hadhrat Abu Bakar (radhiyallahu anhu) and majority of the Sahaabah of Rasulullah

ﷺ. Many of the battles between the Muslims like Jamal, Siffeen and Karbala were instigated by the Shias, who were also active participants in these battles.

Some of the Kufr beliefs of the Shias

The Qur-aan

The Shias believe that the Qur-aan that we have today in our possession is not the Qur-aan that was revealed to Rasulullah ﷺ. They believe that many changes and alterations were made to the Qur-aan before it was handed down to the coming generations. They believe that the Noble Sahaabah (radhiyallahu anhum) made these changes to the Qur-aan Shareef.

The finality of Nubuwat

Shias believe that Nabi ﷺ was not the last and final Nabi of Allah Ta'ala. They have declared that their twelve Imaams are equal in rank to Nabi Muhammad ﷺ.

Nubuwah of Nabi Muhammad ﷺ

The Shias believe that on the Day of Qiyaamah, Rasulullah ﷺ will hand over the banner of praise to Hadhrat Ali (radhiyallahu anhu) and Hadhrat Ali (radhiyallahu anhu) will then

Part One

become the ruler of the entire creation without any exception. They believe that Hadhrat Ali (radhiyallahu anhu) will be even higher than Rasulullah ﷺ (May Allah Ta'ala protect us from such beliefs).

Belief in the Sahaabah ﷺ

The Shias believe that the Sahaabah (radhiyallahu anhum) were all not Muslims but hypocrites and enemies of Allah Ta'ala and Rasulullah ﷺ. They believe that besides Hadhrat Ali (radhiyallahu anhu), Hadhrat Faatimah (radhiyallahu anha), Hadhrat Hasan (radhiyallahu anhu) and Hadhrat Husain (radhiyallahu anhu), Hadhrat Miqdaad (radhiyallahu anhu), Hadhrat Salmaan Faarsi (radhiyallahu anhu), Hadhrat Abu Zarr Ghifaari (radhiyallahu anhu) and a few other Sahaabah, all the other remaining Sahaabah turned away from Islam and became murtad (renegade) (May Allah Ta'ala protect us).

Taqiyyah

Taqiyyah is a doctrine of Shiasm which forms part of the articles of their faith. Taqiyyah means putting up a deceptive appearance or making a statement to hide the truth or mislead the Muslims. In short it means to deceive, lie, or to be a hypocrite. If a Shia uses

Taqiyyah to deceive, fool or betray a Sunni, he will be rewarded for this action of his. In Usoolul Kaafi (a Shia book) it is mentioned that Taqiyyah forms nine tenths (i.e. ninety percent) of the Shia faith. It is also mentioned in their books that Allah Ta'ala will elevate the one who practices Taqiyyah and will disgrace the one who does not practice Taqiyyah.

Mut-ah

Mut-ah means a verbal agreement between a man and a woman to live like husband and wife for a period of time and fixed amount of money. No witnesses are required for such an agreement, nor is it necessary to have anything written down. This agreement can be for one day, one night or even for a few hours. According to the Ahlus Sunnah wal Jama'ah, this is nothing but adultery and prostitution whereas according to the Shias this is an act of righteousness and gains more sawaab than Hajj, Salaah and fasting. In fact it is their belief that any person who does mut-ah once, reaches the position of Hadhrat Hasan (radhiyallahu anhu), if he does it twice he reaches the position of Hadhrat Husain (radhiyallahu anhu), if he does it thrice he reaches the position of Hadhrat Ali (radhiyallahu anhu) and if he does it four times, he reaches the position of Hadhrat Muhammad ﷺ. (Astaghfirallah wa atubu ilayh).

Part One

Contemporary Shiasm

Most of the Shias that exist in todays times are concentrated in Iran, Iraq, Syria, Lebanon, the Middle-East and Far-East countries. Many individuals have migrated to other countries around the world. The Sunnis are not allowed to build Masjids and practice Islam freely in many of the majority Shia countries. The Shia menace and influence lurks in nearly all countries of the world. Innocent and gullible people are sometimes influenced and converted to Shiasm.

Conclusion

Shiasm is a major threat to this Ummah. It is a false religion and has nothing to do with Islam. The only connection to Islam was that the founder of Shiasm, the Jew Abdullah bin Sabah, pretended to be a Muslim thus causing a lot of confusion that Shiasm is part of Islam. They parade as Muslims but they are wolves in sheep clothing. Beware of them as they are detrimental to one's Imaan. May Allah Ta'ala protect us, the Ummah of Rasulullah ﷺ, from the curse of Shiasm and keep us firm on the path of the Sunnah of Rasulullah ﷺ. Similarly, like Shiasm, there are other religions like Qadianism, Bahaiism, Mirzaism, etc. which also claim to be part of Islam but in actual fact has nothing to do with Islam.

Part One

Lessons:

1. Always keep contact with your Utaads, Ulama and pious seniors.
2. If you are in doubt then enquire from your Utaads, Ulama and pious seniors about any new concept, idea or ism that you may be influenced by.
3. Stick to what you learnt under your Ustaaz in madrasah.
4. Any questions and doubts should be referred to your Ustaaz and righteous Ulama. They will always be glad to help you.

Part One

Hadhrat Hasan ﺭﺿﻲﺍﻟﻠﻪﻋﻨﻪ

Hadhrat Hasan (radhiyallahu anhu), the eldest son of Hadhrat Ali (radhiyallahu anhu), was born on 15 Shabaan 3 A.H. He closely resembled his grandfather Rasulullah ﺻﻠﻰﺍﻟﻠﻪﻋﻠﻴﻪﻭﺳﻠﻢ who named him Hasan. Once Rasulullah ﺻﻠﻰﺍﻟﻠﻪﻋﻠﻴﻪﻭﺳﻠﻢ said: "This son of mine is a leader and he will reconcile two large Muslim factions."

Hadhrat Hasan (radhiyallahu anhu) possessed noble character, exercised patience and tolerance and was a very dignified and respectable personality. He was against disunity and bloodshed and tried to maintain peace at all cost. His generosity was also well known. On some occasions he gave away all that he possessed. Hadhrat Hasan (radhiyallahu anhu) had performed Haj twenty-five times on foot.

Appointment as Khalifah

When Hadhrat Ali (radhiyallahu anhu) was on his deathbed, he was consulted about the appointment of Hasan (radhiyallahu anhu) as the next Khalifah to which he replied, "Choose whomsoever you regard suitable."

The people then pledged allegiance to Hadhrat Hasan (radhiyallahu anhu) who then addressed the people as follows;

Part One

"O Muslims, today you have chosen me as your leader, so I expect you to obey me as long as I follow the teachings of the Qur'aan and Hadith. With whoever I make war, you make war and with whoever I make peace you make peace."

During the lifetime of Hadhrat Ali (radhiyallahu anhu), Hadhrat Mu'aawiyah (radhiyallahu anhu) had already taken a pledge with the people of Syria and on hearing about the martyrdom of Hadhrat Ali (radhiyallahu anhu), Hadhrat Mu'aawiyah (radhiyallahu anhu) renewed the pledge and declared himself as the Ameerul Mu'mineen of the Islamic empire.

When Hadhrat Mu'aawiyah (radhiyallahu anhu) heard that the people of Kufa had pledged allegiance to Hadhrat Hasan (radhiyallahu anhu), he prepared an army of 60 000 and left for Kufa. He sent a message to Hasan (radhiyallahu anhu) to accept him as the new Khalifah as this will ensure peace instead of war.

Hadhrat Hasan (radhiyallahu anhu) prepared an army of 40 000 men and then left Kufa to face the army of Hadhrat Mu'aawiyah (radhiyallahu anhu). Hadhrat Hasan (radhiyallahu anhu) addressed the army as follows;

"O people, you had pledged to obey me in war and peace! I take an oath by Almighty Allah that I do not hate anyone. I prefer unity and harmony over disunity and enmity."

Part One

On hearing this speech, the Khawaarij (Kharijites) and the hypocrites, who had treated Ali (radhiyallahu anhu) most despicably, now began to stir trouble against Hasan (radhiyallahu anhu) as they thought that Hasan (radhiyallahu anhu) will enter into a peace agreement with Mu'aawiyah (radhiyallahu anhu) and this will not serve their personal interests. The dissention within the army ranks was brought under control.

Hadhrat Hasan (radhiyallahu anhu) then proceeded with the army to Mada'in where one of the Kharijites attacked him and he was severely wounded. Mu'aawiyah (radhiyallahu anhu) sent a proposal of peace with Abdullah ibn Aamir (radhiyallahu anhu) to Hasan (radhiyallahu anhu). Hasan (radhiyallahu anhu), who had already decided on making peace, strengthened his resolve when he saw the disloyalty of his army.

When Abdullah ibn Aamir (radhiyallahu anhu) brought the proposal of peace, Hadhrat Hasan (radhiyallahu anhu) responded by sending a similar message to Mu'aawiyah (radhiyallahu anhu) adding that he was prepared to accept the proposal on certain conditions, the foremost being that;

- Hadhrat Mu'aawiyah (radhiyallahu anhu) would rule in accordance with the Qur'aan and Hadith.

- Hadhrat Mu'aawiyah (radhiyallahu anhu) must forgive and forget the past differences he had with Ali (radhiyallahu anhu) and Hasan (radhiyallahu anhu), and that he would not confront him or his supporters.

When Mu'aawiyah (radhiyallahu anhu) was informed about Hadhrat Hasan's (radhiyallahu anhu) intentions, he asked Hadhrat Hasan (radhiyallahu anhu) to stipulate any other conditions which he might have. When Husain (radhiyallahu anhu) and Abdullah bin Ja'far (radhiyallahu anhu) learned about Hasan's (radhiyallahu anhu) intention to settle for peace, they were unhappy and tried to convince Hasan (radhiyallahu anhu) to retract his decision. Hasan (radhiyallahu anhu) did not agree as he had already witnessed the disloyalty of the people of Iraq. He was also keen to see the prevailing chaos in the Islamic empire brought to an end and was confident that Hadhrat Mu'aawiyah (radhiyallahu anhu) possessed leadership qualities and was capable to rule the Islamic empire. Hasan (radhiyallahu anhu) therefore went ahead with the peace treaty.

Part One

Peace treaty with Hadhrat Mu'aawiyah ﷺ

Hadhrat Hasan (radhiyallahu anhu) asked his scribe to record the following in the treaty between himself and Mu'aawiyah (radhiyallahu anhu);

1. The Khilaafat will be handed over to Mu'aawiyah bin Abu Sufyaan (radhiyallahu anhu).
2. After the death of Mu'aawiyah (radhiyallahu anhu) the Muslims will elect a new Khalifah.
3. Mu'aawiyah (radhiyallahu anhu) shall treat all Muslims fairly and shall not harm them in any way.
4. Mu'aawiyah (radhiyallahu anhu) shall not harass or confront Hasan (radhiyallahu anhu), Husain (radhiyallahu anhu) and their followers.

Death

Hadhrat Hasan (radhiyallahu anhu) was 47 years old when he passed away in Rabiul Awwal 50 A.H. and was buried next to his mother, Hadhrat Fatima (radhiyallahu anha), in Jannatul Baqi.

Part One

The Umayyad Khilaafat – 95 Years

Even before Islam, the Banu Umayya was a prominent clan. Their leaders were famous for their qualities of leadership, foresight, developing strategies and politics. During the Umayyad Khilaafat, many territories came under the Umayyad rule, and the Empire expanded considerably. Yemen, Armenia, Azerbaijan, Eastern Asia, North Africa, etc. came under the Umayyad rule. The following is a list of the Umayyad leaders;

NO	RULERS	SEAT OF RULE	PERIOD
1	Hadhrat Mu'aawiyah رضي الله عنه	Damascus	41 to 60 A.H.
2	Yazeed bin Mu'aawiyah	Damascus	60 to 63 A.H.
3	Mu'aawiyah bin Yazeed	Damascus	63 A.H.
4	Marwan bin Hakam	Damascus	63 to 65 A.H.
5	Abdul Malik bin Marwaan	Damascus	65 to 86 A.H.
	Abdullah bin Zubair رضي الله عنه not part of the Umayyad Dynasty	Makkah	68 to 73 A.H.
6	Walid bin Abdul Malik	Damascus	86 to 96 A.H.
7	Sulaiman bin Abdul Malik	Damascus	96 to 99 A.H.
8	Umar bin Abdul Aziz (rahmatullahi alayh)	Damascus	99 to 101 A.H.
9	Yazeed bin Abdul Malik	Damascus	101 to 105 A.H.
10	Hishaam bin Abdul Malik	Damascus	105 to 125 A.H.

Part One

11	Walid bin Yazeed	Damascus	125 A.H.
12	Yazeed bin Walid	Damascus	126 to 127 A.H.
13	Ibrahim bin Walid	Damascus	127 to 132 A.H.
14	Marwan bin Muhammad bin Marwaan	Damascus	132 to 135 A.H.

1. The Umayyad Khilaafat consisted of fourteen leaders and lasted for approximately ninety five years starting from the year 661 C.E. (41 A.H.) to 750 C.E. (132 A.H.).
2. Although Hadhrat Uthmaan (radhiyallahu anhu) was from among the Banu Umayya, the actual Umayyad Khilaafat started from the Khilaafat of Hadhrat Mu'aawiyah (radhiyallahu anhu). **Abdullah bin Zubair** (radhiyallahu anhu) **was not part of the Umayyad Dynasty.**
3. The Umayyads were the descendants of Umayya, the grandfather of Hadhrat Uthmaan (radhiyallahu anhu).
4. The practice of appointing a family member as the head of state was initiated by the Banu Umayya and subsequently continued by the Abbaasid khilaafat.
5. The Umayyad Khilaafat was based in Damascus.
6. The most prominent Khulafa in the Umayyad dynasty were Hadhrat Mu'aawiyah (radhiyallahu anhu), Abdul Malik bin Marwaan, Walid bin Abdul Malik and Hadhrat Umar bin Abdul Aziz (rahmatullahi alayh).

Achivements of the Banu Umayya

1. A formal army was established and military equipment was acquired.
2. Kufa and Basrah became the two centres of learning and the study of Qur'aan and Hadith was undertaken.
3. A postal system with riders on horseback was established.
4. Currency in the form of the Dinar and Dirham was introduced.
5. The Arabic language spread to all parts of the Empire.

Part One

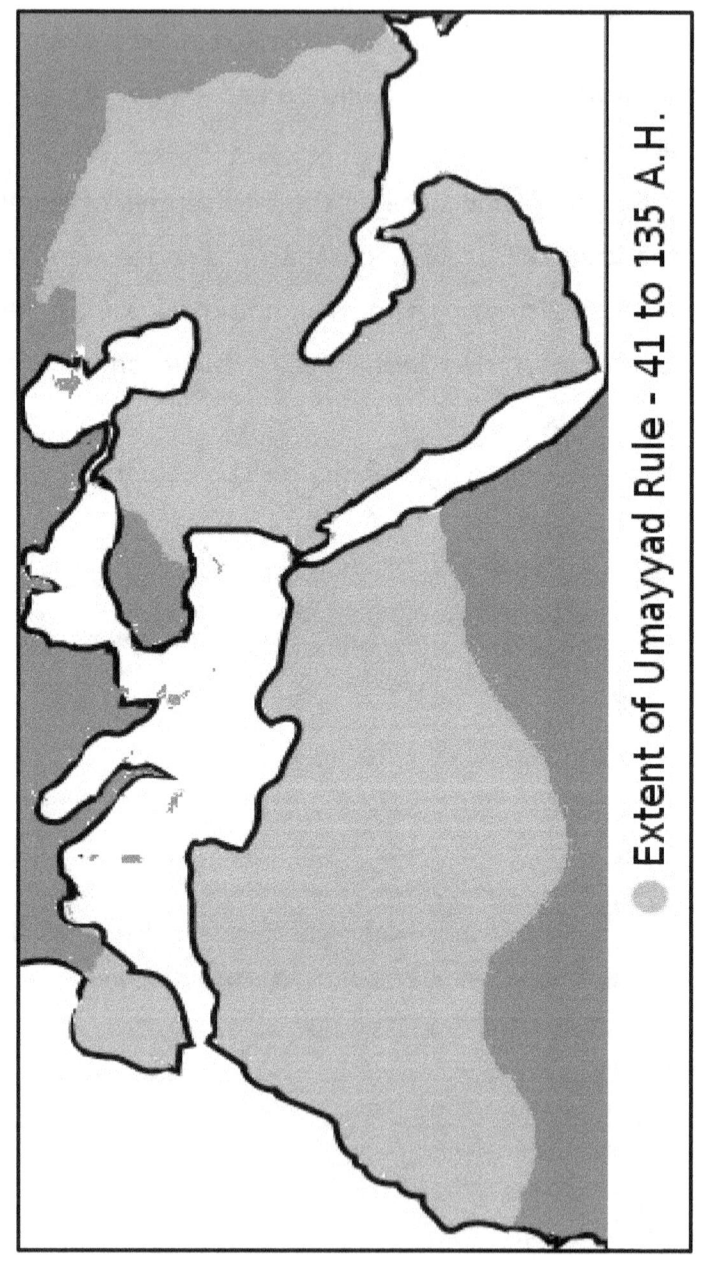

Part One

Hadhrat Mu'aawiyah رضى الله عنه

Hadhrat Mu'aawiyah (radhiyallahu anhu) was born seventeen years before the advent of Hijrat. His father's name was Abu Sufyaan and his mother's name was Hindah. Mu'aawiyah (radhiyallahu anhu) and his father both embraced Islam on the conquest of Makkah. At that time Mu'aawiyah (radhiyallahu anhu) was twenty-five years of age and since then remained in the company of Rasulullah ﷺ.

Hadhrat Mu'aawiyah (radhiyallahu anhu) possessed an overwhelming stature, a youthful complexion and a handsome face. Even in his childhood days he displayed leadership qualities for which the people called him the "Kisra of the Arabs" (which refers to his leadership qualities). His tolerance, generosity, wisdom, foresight, love for peace and justice was known not only by the Muslims but also the Kuffaar.

Before Islam he did not participate in any battle against the Muslims. He was chosen as a scribe to record Wahi and also to attend to groups of representatives, from different lands and tribes, which came to Rasulullah ﷺ in Madinah. He narrated 160 Ahaadith.

Part One

During the Khilaafat of Hadhrat Abu Bakr (radhiyallahu anhu), Hadhrat Mu'aawiyah (radhiyallahu anhu) led the army which went to Syria (Shaam). Hadhrat Umar (radhiyallahu anhu) appointed Hadhrat Mu'aawiyah (radhiyallahu anhu) as the Governor of Jordan and surrounding areas. He was the Governor of Syria (Shaam) for twenty-five years, and when he was declared Khalifah, he held this post for another twenty-five years. Rasulullah ﷺ prophesised his Khilaafat when he once said to him: **"When you become a ruler, treat the people with kindness."**

On becoming the Khalifah, the first major problem for Hadhrat Mu'aawiyah (radhiyallahu anhu) was to deal with the internal strife in the Islamic Empire. All the different groups and the rebels were brought under control and there was peace in the Islamic Empire. Hadhrat Mu'aawiyah (radhiyallahu anhu) appointed capable governors in the different provinces and cities, who helped to bring about law and order in the Islamic Empire.

When the internal strife was brought under control, Hadhrat Mu'aawiyah (radhiyallahu anhu) decided to deal with the external threats to the Islamic Empire. The harassment of the Kuffaar and the threat of the Roman navy, which carried out attacks on areas under Muslim rule, were brought under control. Hadhrat Mu'aawiyah (radhiyallahu anhu) strengthened the naval and defence forces and established naval bases in nearby islands like Cyprus.

Expedition to Constantinople (Istanbul)

The Romans constantly launched attacks from Constantinople. Hadhrat Mu'aawiyah (radhiyallahu anhu) wanted to remove all future threats to the Islamic Empire, so he ordered an attack on the main Roman base, which was Constantinople.

Volunteers were called from the entire Islamic Empire and many volunteers including senior Sahaabah like Abdullah bin Zubair, Abdullah bin Abbas, Husain bin Ali and Abu Ayyub Ansari (radhiyallahu anhum) participated in the expedition as they had not forgotten the prophesy of Rasulullah ﷺ:

"The first army of my Ummah which will advance upon the city of the Romans will be forgiven."

Soon a massive army including a naval fleet was sent to Constantinople. Due to the city being fortified by a huge wall, the army could not penetrate. Many Sahaabah, including Hadhrat Abu Ayyub Ansari (radhiyallahu anhu), were martyred and buried here.

Part One

Due to the cold weather and other obstacles, Constantinople could not be conquered and the Muslim army returned. After this expedition the Romans did not provoke the Muslims.

Summary of the Achievements of Hadhrat Mu'aawiyah's رضي الله عنه Khilaafat

Hadhrat Mu'aawiyah (radhiyallahu anhu) held the position of Khalifah for twenty-five years, which was a very successful period in the history of Islam for the following reasons;

1. No part of the Islamic Empire was lost but rather it expanded in all directions. There was no civil unrest during this period.
2. No rebellion or uprising against the governors in any of the provinces was reported. The instability and chaos that previously prevailed was eradicated.
3. Hadhrat Mu'aawiyah (radhiyallahu anhu) was the first person to build warships in the history of Islam and the Islamic navy was established, thereby subduing the Roman threat.
4. The Iranian and Iraqi threat was brought under control.
5. The placing of official seals on all important correspondences was introduced.

6. The first ever postal system in an organised way was introduced.
7. Security arrangements were introduced by placing guards at the doors of important people.

Hadhrat Mu'aawiyah (radhiyallahu anhu) and Hadhrat Ali (radhiyallahu anhu) had certain differences between them which were based totally on the Haq (truth) and not on personal differences. They both intended well for the betterment of Deen and each took steps based on Haq for the upliftment of Deen.

The succession of Hadhrat Mu'aawiyah رضى الله عنه

Hadhrat Mu'aawiyah (radhiyallahu anhu), who was diligently running the Islamic empire, did not give any thought about his successor until Hadhrat Mughirah bin Shu'bah (radhiyallahu anhu), the governor of Kufa, brought up the subject. Hadhrat Mughirah bin Shu'bah (radhiyallahu anhu) suggested that in order to avoid bloodshed, Hadhrat Mu'aawiyah (radhiyallahu anhu) should appoint his son Yazeed in his lifetime.

Hadhrat Mu'aawiyah (radhiyallahu anhu) also thought that Yazeed would ensure the smooth running of the Islamic empire. Hadhrat Mughirah bin Shu'bah (radhiyallahu anhu) convinced the people of Kufa but Marwaan bin Hakam, the governor of Madinah, could not convince the senior Sahaabah who opposed the nomination of Yazeed. Hadhrat Abdur Rahmaan bin Abu Bakr, Abdullah bin Umar, Abdullah bin Zubair and Husain bin Ali (radhiyallahu anhum) were amongst those who rejected the nomination of Yazeed. Subsequently Mughirah bin Shu'ba (radhiyallahu anhu) who initiated the idea of succession passed away.

By the year 56 A.H., except for the few senior Sahaabah (radhiyallahu anhum), most of the Islamic Empire had pledged their allegiance to Yazeed as the next Khalifah.

Death of Hadhrat Mu'aawiyah (radhiyallahu anhu)

In Rajab, the 60th year A.H., Hadhrat Mu'aawiyah (radhiyallahu anhu) took ill and three weeks later, on the 22nd Rajab, at the age of seventy, he passed away.

Hadhrat Abdullah bin Zubair ﷺ

(Not part of the Umayyad Dynasty) Makkah 68 to 73 A.H.

Hadhrat Abdullah bin Zubair (radhiyallahu anhu), who was very handsome, was the son of the great Sahaabi Hadhrat Zubair bin Awaam (radhiyallahu anhu). His mother was Asma (radhiyallahu anha), the daughter of Hadhrat Abu Bakr (radhiyallahu anhu). Hadhrat Abdullah bin Zubair (radhiyallahu anhu) was the first child to be born to the Muhaajireen and Rasulullah ﷺ made "Tahneek" for him.

He performed Salaah and fasted abundantly in his youth and on occasions, stood in Salaah the entire night. He was an expert horseman and a brave warrior. He led a life of abstinence and piety and was the last Sahaabi who ruled by example.

After the demise of Hadhrat Mu'aawiyah (radhiyallahu anhu), there was tremendous opposition to the Khilaafat of Yazeed. The correct choice was Hadhrat Abdullah bin Zubair (radhiyallahu anhu) as he was acceptable to most of the people. The only opposition to his khilaafat was the Banu Umayyah. The martyrdom of Hadhrat Husain (radhiyallahu anhu), strengthened the opposition to Yazeed's khilaafat.

Part One

Hadhrat Abdullah bin Zubair (radhiyallahu anhu) was declared Governor of Makkah in the early stages of Yazeed's Khilaafat as the people of Makkah did not acknowledge Yazeed's Khilaafat. Yazeed had even sent an army to Makkah which returned unsuccessful. After the battle of Karbala, Hadhrat Abdullah bin Zubair (radhiyallahu anhu) was declared Khalifah of the Islamic Empire by the people of Makkah, Basra and Egypt. In 68 A.H., Kufa also came under the rule of Hadhrat Abdullah bin Zubair (radhiyallahu anhu).

Hadhrat Abdullah bin Zubair (radhiyallahu anhu) could not bring the areas of Shaam and Palestine under his control. These areas were controlled by Abdul Malik bin Marwaan of the Banu Umayya. In 70 A.H., Abdul Malik bin Marwaan succeeded in bringing most of the areas controlled by Abdullah bin Zubair (radhiyallahu anhu) under his rule. In 72 A.H., Abdul Malik bin Marwaan ordered his Governor, Hajjaj bin Yusuf Saqafi, to prepare for war against Hadhrat Abdullah bin Zubair (radhiyallahu anhu) in Makkah.

A siege was laid upon Makkah and attacks were launched by the assistance of a huge catapult on Jabal Abu Qubais, which overlooks the Ka'bah. The attacks were launched in Ramadhaan and continued in the months of Haj. The people who had come for Haj completed the rituals of Haj with much difficulty. Hadhrat Abdullah bin Zubair (radhiyallahu anhu) was prevented from performing Haj and could barely manage to perform Salaah in the Haram Shareef.

Martydom of Hadhrat Abdullah bin Zubair (radhiyallahu anhu)

The siege around Makkah began taking its toll on the Makkans who faced a shortage of supplies. Many of Hadhrat Abdullah bin Zubair's (radhiyallahu anhu) supporters lost morale and crossed into Hajjaj's camp. With no support left, Hadhrat Abdullah bin Zubair (radhiyallahu anhu) was asked to surrender.

Hadhrat Abdullah bin Zubair (radhiyallahu anhu) asked his mother for advice in the prevailing circumstances. She advised him to remain steadfast and to seek the help of Allah Ta'ala in all his affairs. She told him that, "You too will be honoured with martyrdom like many of your supporters". Hadhrat Abdullah bin Zubair (radhiyallahu anhu) replied; "This is what I always wanted. I never desired power or wealth. I merely accepted this position so that I may encourage people to obey Allah's commandments and prevent them from His disobedience."

His mother bid him farewell and he left to face the enemy. With few of his loyal supporters, he launched an attack and the battle continued for most of the day. In spite of his bravery, he was overpowered by the army of Hajjaj and was martyred on 11th Jumadul Ukhra 73 A.H. His rule lasted for 13 years. Since the

Part One

khilaafat of Abdullah bin Zubair (radhiyallahu anhu) was plagued by internal strife, there was no expansion in the Islamic Empire during his rule.

Part One

Yazeed bin Mu'aawiyah

Yazeed bin Mu'aawiyah was born in 25 A.H. when his father was governor of Sham (Syria). He was raised up in the house of the Khalifah and was fortunate to be educated in various fields. He was appointed as Ameer for Haj on a few occasions and was one of the commanders of the Constantinople expedition.

Appointment to Khilaafat

Most of the people of Shaam and the governors of the different provinces renewed their pledge to Yazeed after the demise of Hadhrat Mu'aawiyah (radhiyallahu anhu). In Madinah, Hadhrat Husain (radhiyallahu anhu) withheld his pledge and requested for time to think the matter over.

The second prominent person who was opposed to the appointment of Yazeed was Hadhrat Abdullah bin Zubair (radhiyallahu anhu). Both Hadhrat Husain (radhiyallahu anhu) and Hadhrat Abdullah bin Zubair (radhiyallahu anhu) were being pressurised into accepting Yazeed, as a result of which they left Madinah Munawarah secretly and went to Makkah Mukaramah. The senior Ulama and the general public of Makkah pledged allegiance to Hadhrat Abdullah bin Zubair (radhiyallahu anhu), who took over the governorship of Makkah Mukaramah. Yazeed

Part One

sent an army to Makkah Mukaramah to arrest Hadhrat Abdullah bin Zubair (radhiyallahu anhu) but the army returned unsuccessful.

Events leading to the Battle of Karbala

The people of Kufa invited Hadhrat Husain (radhiyallahu anhu) to Kufa, promising to pledge allegiance to him and support him. Hadhrat Husain (radhiyallahu anhu) remembered the words of his brother Hadhrat Hasan (radhiyallahu anhu); **"Do not be deceived by the people of Kufa"**. After much hesitance, he accepted the request and finally responded when he was informed that 12 000 people had pledged support for him. He also sent an envoy to Basra to get the support of the people of Basra.

Yazeed sent Ubaidullah bin Ziyaad with a huge army to Kufa to stop the people pledging support for Hadhrat Husain (radhiyallahu anhu). Hadhrat Husain (radhiyallahu anhu) was still in Makkah at this time. Ubaidullah addressed the people and warned them that should they oppose him and side with Hadhrat Husain (radhiyallahu anhu), they will be killed. Ubaidullah also had the envoys of Hadhrat Husain (radhiyallahu anhu) executed in front of the people. The people were fearful of Ubaidullah and began to disperse silently. Yazeed informed Ubaidullah that Hadhrat Husain (radhiyallahu anhu) had left Makkah and was on his way to Kufa.

Ubaidullah was ordered to prevent Hadhrat Husain (radhiyallahu anhu) from entering Kufa.

Hadhrat Husain (radhiyallahu anhu) was unaware that his envoy has been killed and the people of Kufa had withdrawn their support due to the fear of the tyranny of Ubaidullah. Senior Sahaabah, like Hadhrat Abdullah bin Umar (radhiyallahu anhu) and Hadhrat Abdullah bin Abbas (radhiyallahu anhu), tried to advise Hadhrat Husain (radhiyallahu anhu) not to proceed to Kufa, reminding him about the manner the people of Kufa treated his father and brother. They also advised him not to take his family with. Hadhrat Abdullah bin Zubair (radhiyallahu anhu) also tried to stop Hadhrat Husain (radhiyallahu anhu) from going to Kufa by offering him the governorship of Makkah. But Hadhrat Husain (radhiyallahu anhu) was determined and no amount of pressure was going to stop him from going to Kufa.

Part One

Route taken by Hadhrat Husain ﷺ from Madinah Munawwarah to Kufa

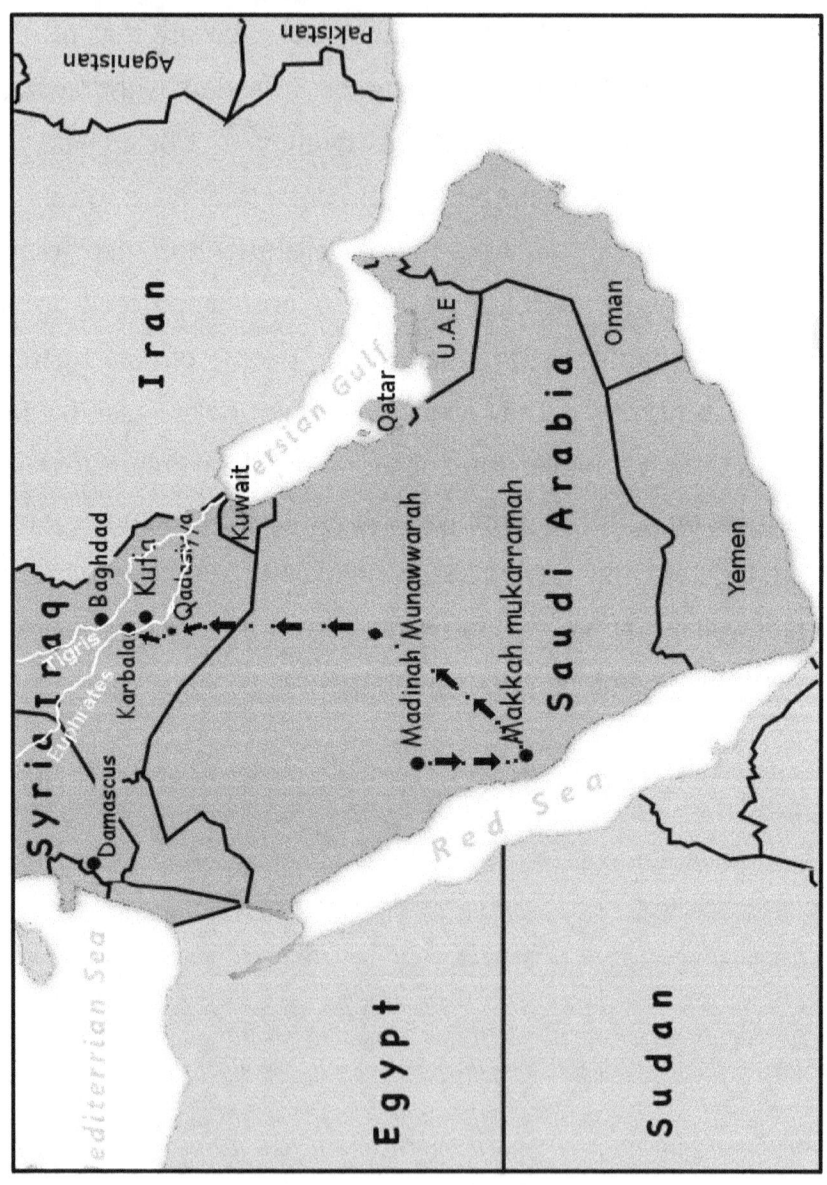

Finally on 3rd Zul Hijjah, 60 A.H., Hadhrat Husain (radhiyallahu anhu) left for Kufa, unaware that on that very day his envoy was martyred. In Kufa, Ubaidullah was preparing a huge army to prevent Hadhrat Husain (radhiyallahu anhu) from entering. Before entering Kufa, Hadhrat Husain (radhiyallahu anhu) sent a messenger ahead to inform the people of his arrival. The messenger was killed by Ubaidullah's men. A second messenger was sent and met the same fate. Hadhrat Husain (radhiyallahu anhu) was unaware of the killing of his messengers.

When Hadhrat Husain (radhiyallahu anhu) reached near Kufa, then only did he receive the news that his two messengers were killed. He also became aware that Ubaidullah was the governor and the people were too afraid to stand up to him. He also came to know that his envoy to Kufa was martyred. This terrible news was a severe blow to the morale of Hadhrat Husain (radhiyallahu anhu) and his army. They were in a strange land and they did not know what to do next.

The various tribes that joined Hadhrat Husain (radhiyallahu anhu) along the way now began deserting him and he was left with seventy to eighty men only. Against all odds they proceeded towards Kufa to avenge the death of their envoy but en-route they were blocked by the army of Ubaidullah. When Hadhrat Husain (radhiyallahu anhu) realised that his entry into Kufa was blocked by

Part One

the same people who had called him to Kufa, he decided to turn back and return. When he turned back to return, he was prevented from doing so. He now turned towards Qaadisiyyah with Ubaidullah's men in pursuit.

Hadhrat Husain (radhiyallahu anhu) learnt that another army, under the leadership of Amr Ibn Saad, was waiting for him on the outskirts of the city, so he once again changed his route until he reached Karbala which is about sixteen kilometres from Qaadisiyyah. Amr asked Hadhrat Husain (radhiyallahu anhu) to abandon the idea of becoming the Kalifah and he will be free to go, otherwise he will be arrested as per the instructions of Ubaidullah. Hadhrat Husain (radhiyallahu anhu) put the following three proposals forward to Amr;

1. To allow him to return to Makkah Mukaramah and engross himself in the Ibaadat of Allah Ta'ala.   OR
2. To allow him to proceed to the Islamic borders to wage jihaad and gain martyrdom.   OR
3. To allow him to proceed to Shaam and discuss matters with Yazeed personally.

Amr Ibn Sa'ad sent the proposals to Ubaidullah, who wanted to accept one of the proposals but one of his close advisers advised him to reject them. Ubaidullah's advisor advised him to ask Hadhrat Husain (radhiyallahu anhu) to pledge allegiance to Yazeed at Ubaidullah's hands. Hadhrat Husain (radhiyallahu anhu) rejected this unreasonable proposal. An entire week passed with negotiations between both parties whilst they were encamped at Karbala. There was a cordial and friendly atmosphere with both parties even performing Salaah behind one another.

When Ubaidullah came to know of this, he reprimanded Amr and ordered him to arrest Hadhrat Husain (radhiyallahu anhu) or to kill him and send him his head. On Thursday evening, the 9th of Muharram, Amr informed Hadhrat Husain (radhiyallahu anhu) of the order of Ubaidullah. Husain (radhiyallahu anhu) requested Amr to postpone the battle for the next day saying, "I will have made my decision by tomorrow," to which Amr agreed.

Ubaidullah also sent reinforcements to Karbala and also sent a message that if the battle had not commenced as yet, then Husain (radhiyallahu anhu) should not be allowed to draw water from the Euphrates River, on the banks of which both armies were camped. Five hundred men were posted on the banks of the river to prevent the army of Husain (radhiyallahu anhu) from drawing water. The entire group of Husain (radhiyallahu anhu), including women and children, were prevented from quenching their thirst the entire night and the following night as well.

Part One

The Battle of Karbala

On Friday morning, the 10th of Muharram, Hadhrat Husain's (radhiyallahu anhu) group of seventy to eighty men faced Ubaidullah's army of a few thousand men. Hadhrat Husain (radhiyallahu anhu) addressed the enemy thus;

"You are aware that I am the grandson of Rasulullah ﷺ and the son of Hadhrat Ali (radhiyallahu anhu) and Faatimah (radhiyallahu anha). My brother and I have been given the glad tidings by Rasulullah ﷺ of being the leaders of the youth in Jannah. I have never broken a promise or delayed a Salaah. I have neither harmed nor killed any Muslim. If the donkey of Isa (alayhis salaam) were to be alive today, the Christians would have taken care of it till the Day of Qiyaamah. I am the grandson of Rasulullah ﷺ, and you have no shame that you are prepared to kill me today? I was at peace in Makkah and Madinah, but you did not allow me to rest. You persistently called me to come to you, and you promised me your full support. But here you are today, ready with your swords drawn over me."

Hadhrat Husain (radhiyallahu anhu) read out the letters sent to him by the various leaders but they denied having written to him. The battle then began and the small army of Hadhrat Husain (radhiyallahu anhu) fought valiantly but eventually succumbed and were crowned with martyrdom. Finally, Hadhrat Husain (radhiyallahu anhu) was also martyred and the women and children were taken captive. The only surviving male member was Ali, the young son of Hadhrat Husain (radhiyallahu anhu), known as Zainul Abedeen.

Ubaidullah then sent the entire family of Hadhrat Husain (radhiyallahu anhu) to Yazeed in Damascus. They presented the head of Hadhrat Husain (radhiyallahu anhu) to Yazeed, who was utterly shocked and devastated, and wept uncontrollably. Yazeed reprimanded those who had come with the head of Hadhrat Husain (radhiyallahu anhu) and cursed Ubaidullah and the others who were responsible in slaying the grandson of Rasulullah ﷺ. Yazeed immediately released the family of Hadhrat Husain (radhiyallahu anhu). He hosted them at his house with respect and thereafter sent them to Madinah Munawarah, promising to assist them. Ubaidullah thought that by slaying Hadhrat Husain (radhiyallahu anhu), he would attain the favour of Yazeed, but was disappointed at the reaction of Yazeed. Instead of pleasing Yazeed, he was disgraced and humiliated.

On hearing about the murder of Hadhrat Husain (radhiyallahu anhu), Hadhrat Abdullah bin Zubair (radhiyallahu anhu) was extremely grieved and called for the removal of Yazeed. The people of Makkah now declared Hadhrat Abdullah bin Zubair

Part One

(radhiyallahu anhu) as the Khalifah of the Islamic Empire. In response to this, Yazeed ordered an attack on Makkah Mukaramah but was unsuccessful. He thereafter attacked Madinah Munawarah and overpowered the people of Madinah.

A siege was laid upon Makkah and attacks were launched by the assistance of a huge catapult on Jabal Abu Qubais, which overlooks the Ka'bah. The attacks were launched in Ramadhaan and continued in the months of Haj. While the battle raged, news was received on the 10th Rabiul Awwal 64 A.H. that Yazeed had passed away in Shaam. He was thirty-eight years old and ruled for three years and eight months.

The commander of Yazeed's army asked Abdullah bin Zubair (radhiyallahu anhu) to take over the Khilaafat but he refused. When passing by Madinah, the commander asked Hadhrat Zainul Abedeen to take over the Khilaafat but he also refused asking to be left alone as he had taken a vow with Allah Ta'ala never to take up leadership.

Yazeed's Successor

Due to internal strife in the Islamic Empire, there was very little expansion under Yazeed. After Yazeed's demise his son Abdur Rahman bin Yazeed was appointed as Khalifah. Abdur Rahman was a man of upright character and led an extremely pious life. He was a very sickly person and passed away only three months into his Khilaafat.

Abdul Malik bin Marwaan
73 to 86 A.H. (13 Years)

Abdul Malik bin Marwaan became Khalifah after the martyrdom of Abdullah bin Zubair (radhiyallahu anhu). Hajjaj bin Yusuf was appointed as governor of Hejaz. Hajjaj's tyranny, which is well known, affected many people including senior Sahaabah (radhiyallahu anhum). Hajjaj was later appointed governor of Kufa.

During the reign of Abdul Malik bin Marwaan, the first Islamic coins were minted. He managed to strengthen the Umayyad Dynasty during the thirteen years of his rule. He passed away in 86 A.H. and his son Waleed succeeded him.

Waleed bin Abdul Malik
86 to 96 A.H. (10 Years)

After the demise of his father, Abdul Malik bin Marwaan, Waleed bin Abdul Malik took over the Khilaafat. Waleed appointed Umar bin Abdul Aziz (rahmatullahi alayh) as Governor of Madinah

Part One

Munawarah. After Waleed's demise in 96 A.H., his brother Sulaiman was appointed Khalifah. Sulaiman was martyred in 99 A.H. while engaging in Jihaad and was succeeded by Umar bin Abdul Aziz (rahmatullahi alayh).

Umar bin Abdul Aziz رحمه الله
99 to 101 A.H. (2 Years)

Umar bin Abdul Aziz (rahmatullahi alayh) was born in the year 62 A.H. His father was Abdul Aziz bin Marwan, who was the governor of Egypt. His mother, Fathima, was the granddaughter of Hadhrat Umar (radhiyallahu anhu) and daughter of Hadhrat Aasim (radhiyallahu anhu). In his childhood, Umar bin Abdul Aziz (rahmatullahi alayh) was injured by a horse, which caused a scar on his face. Hadhrat Umar (radhiyallahu anhu) once remarked that from his progeny a person with a scarred face will fill the earth with his just rule.

In his childhood, Umar bin Abdul Aziz (rahmatullahi alayh) was sent to Madinah Munawarah by his father to receive education. He spent time in the company of the pious and learned Ulama from a young age, which resulted in him acquiring a deep understanding of Deen.

Part One

Appointment as governor and Khalifah

He was appointed governor of Madinah from 86 A.H. – 96 A.H., prior to becoming Khalifah in 96 A.H. The father of Umar bin Abdul Aziz (rahmatullahi alayh) was nominated to succeed Abdul Malik bin Marwaan but passed away before Abdul Malik bin Marwaan. Walid bin Abdul Malik succeeded Abdul Malik bin Marwaan and Sulaiman bin Abdul Malik followed. Sulaiman bin Abdul Malik sealed the name of the next Khalifah in an envelope, which was opened after his death and the contents declared Umar bin Abdul Aziz (rahmatullahi alayh) as the next Khalifah.

Umar bin Abdul Aziz (rahmatullahi alayh) was shocked and not happy at his appointment, but was forcibly placed on the pulpit and the people pledged allegiance to him. His wife asked why he was crying and he replied that the burden of the Ummat has been placed on him and he had to account for this on the day of Qiyaamah. He asked his wife to place all her jewellery in the public treasury or otherwise be separated from him. His wife gladly accepted his request. When she was offered back the jewels after the demise of her husband, she refused.

When Umar bin Abdul Aziz (rahmatullahi alayh) took up the khilaafat, he addressed the people thus; "O people, there is no book besides the Qur'aan and no nabi after Muhammad ﷺ.

Part One

I am not here to start anything new, but only to complete my task. I am not a founder, but rather a follower. I am in no way better than you, but I am carrying a heavier burden than you." He then continued: "Remember, it is not permissible to obey anyone if such obedience results in the disobedience of the orders of the Creator."

After taking the pledge of allegiance he was offered a state horse to ride on, which he refused and replied, "My mule is sufficient for me." He asked the caretaker to sell all the horses used for those in power and use the money for the needs of the poor. He was told to reside in the residence of the Khalifah but decided to continue living in his tent. He ruled over his subjects like a compassionate father and he was adored by all his subjects, Muslims and non-Muslims.

Simplicity and popularity

Before becoming Khalifah, he wore very expensive clothes but when he assumed the post of khilafat, he wore very simple and cheap clothing. He could have lived like a king, but on numerous occasions he was seen leading the Salaah with patched clothing and he had become so lean that the bones of his body were clearly visible. When Umar bin Abdul Aziz (rahmatullahi alayh) took up the khilaafat, there were over hundred guards to protect the Khalifah.

He dismissed all of them saying, "My safety is decided by taqdeer, therefore I have no need for guards."

Death

Certain people from the ruling class were unable to fulfil their own greed and ambitions because of Umar bin Abdul Aziz's (rahmatullahi alayh) just rule and strict adherence to the Shariah. So they assassinated him by bribing a slave to poison his food.

During his rule there was such peace and harmony that even the wolves would not attack the sheep. Once, when a wolf attacked a sheep, a shepherd remarked that; "Our pious Khalifah has passed away". When he died, his estate consisted of twenty-one dinars from which his funeral expenses were paid and the remainder was distributed amongst his heirs. Not only did the Muslims mourn his death, but the Christians, Jews and followers of other religions as well. He had three wives and eleven children.

Part One

Muhammad bin Qaasim

The areas of Sindh, Baluchistan, etc. were close to the borders of Kufa and provided a safe haven for the enemies of the Islamic state. The ruler of Sindh also assisted the enemies of the Islamic state in times of war. Hajjaj bin Yusuf, the governor of one of the provinces, sent an army to deal with the ruler of Sindh. One of the commanders of the Muslim army was Muhammad bin Qaasim Saqafi, a seventeen year old youth who was also the son-in-law of Hajjaj.

Muhammed bin Qaasim conquered these hostile areas of Sindh, etc. Muhammad bin Qaasim also conquered parts of India by 96 A.H. In 95 A.H. Hajjaj passed away. Muhammad bin Qaasim, who was an extremely kind, just and merciful ruler, treated his subjects with great compassion. He was a leader with exceptional qualities and of noble character. He was extremely dedicated to his mission and his soldiers and subjects loved him and gave him loyal support. Due to his noble qualities, his fame spread in the Muslim Empire.

Part One

Conquest of Spain

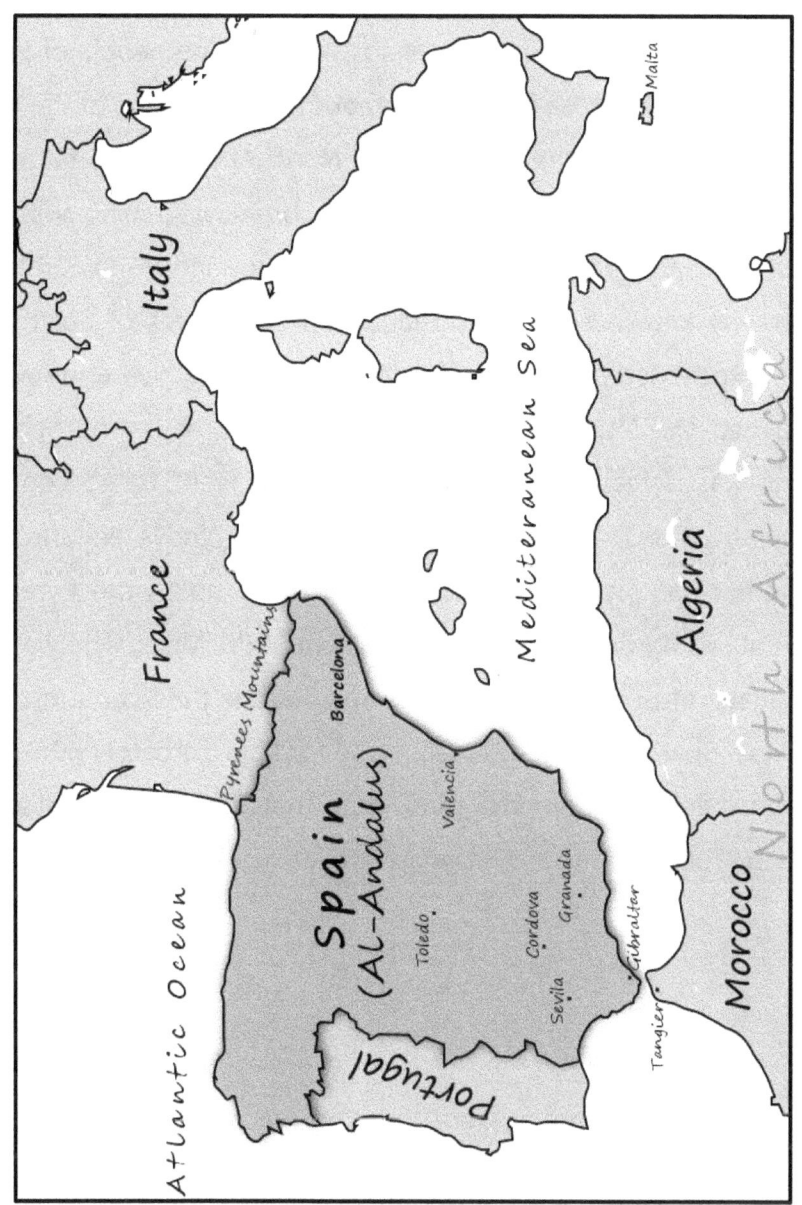

51

Part One

Conquest of Spain - 92 A.H.

Roderick, the king of Spain, was a cruel ruler. The people of Spain complained to Moosa bin Nazeer about the oppression of the king. Moosa bin Nazeer, the conqueror of North Africa, sent an army to Spain under the command of Taariq bin Ziyaad who was the governor of Tangiers. Taariq bin Ziyaad landed in Gibraltar (formerly known as Jabalut Taariq), on the shores of Spain and then proceeded north, were he confronted a massive army which engaged the Muslims in battle, lasting eight days. The Spanish army was defeated and Taariq bin Ziyaad went on to conquer other areas of Spain. He was joined by Moosa bin Nazeer and they together conquered the rest of Spain right up to the Pyrenees Mountains bordering France. Waleed bin Abdul Malik, who was the Khalifah, refused them permission to continue their conquest into Europe. Spain was under Muslim rule for approximately 800 years and was lost at about the same time that the Abbasid Khilaafat, which followed the Umayyad Khilaafat, came to an end.

Part Two

PART TWO

The Abbasid Khilaafat

1. With the fall of the Umayyad Khilaafat, the Abbasids became rulers of the Muslim Empire.
2. The Abbasids were the descendants of Hadhrat Abbas bin Abdul Muttalib (radhiyallahu anhu), the paternal uncle of Rasulullah ﷺ.
3. The Abbasid Khilaafat provided 37 leaders and lasted for approximately 508 years starting from the year 750 C.E. (132 A.H.) to 1258 C.E. (656 A.H.).
4. The Abbasid Khilaafat was based in Baghdad and Kufa.
5. This period also saw many advances in secular subjects such as algebra, astronomy, medicine and other related scientific fields.
6. The Abbasid Khilaafat began with Abul Abbaas As Saffah in 750 C.E. and ended in 1258 C.E. when they were conquered by the Mongols.
7. Many historians divide the Abbasid Khilaafat in two periods. The first of the two periods 132 A.H. – 227 A.H. (750 C.E. to 845 C.E.) was known as the golden age which saw prosperity and the empire at its peak, whilst the second period 233 A.H. – 656 A.H. (846 C.E. to 1258 C.E.) saw the

slow decline and demise of the dynasty, with the Muslims being threatened from within and outside forces.

Although the Abbasid Khilaafat provided 37 leaders, only the following five will be discussed;

NO	RULERS	PERIOD
1	Abul Abbaas As Saffah	132 to 136 A.H.
2	Mansur	137 to 159 A.H.
5	Haroon Ar-Rasheed	170 to 194 A.H.
6	Muhammad Al-Ameen bin Haroon	194 to 198 A.H.
7	Ma'mun Ar-Rasheed	198 to 218 A.H.

Part Two

Extent of the Abbasid Empire

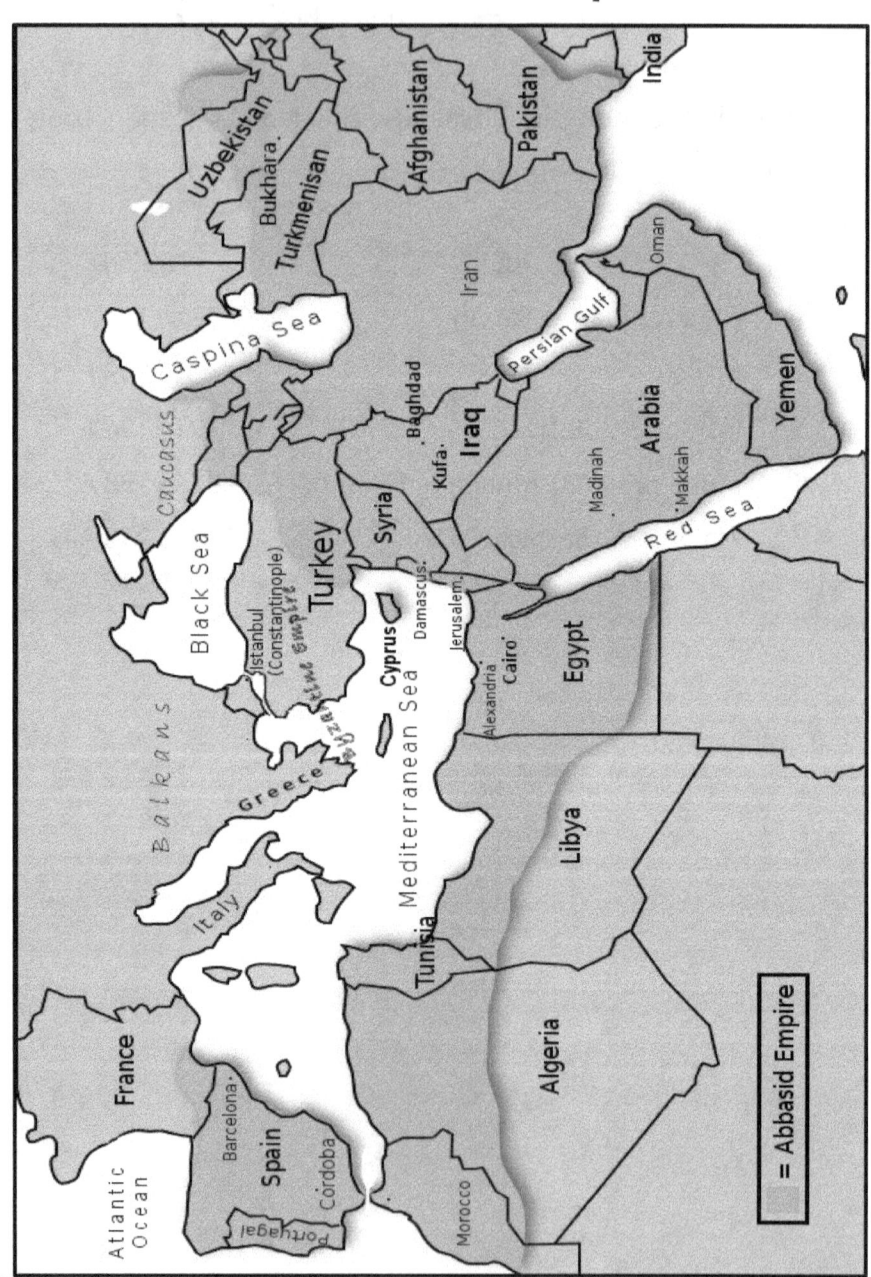

Abul Abbaas As Saffah

The Abbasids fought in the battle known as **'The Great Zab'** and defeated the Umayyads. The Abbasids took over the Khilaafat and the first Khalifah of the Abbasid Dynasty was Abul Abbaas As Saffah (the title 'As Saffah' means 'blood shedder'). The people were forced to submit to the Abbasid rule and in the process many people were massacred or imprisoned. The capital of the Islamic Empire was moved from Damascus to Kufa.

During his rule, Abul Abbaas was responsible for extending the Muslim Empire. Abul Abbaas As Saffah died of small pox in 754 C.E.

Mansur

Abu Jafar Abdullah, also popularly known as Mansur 'the victorious', succeeded his brother Abul Abbaas As Saffah. Upon his ascension, his uncle Abdullah bin Ali also laid claim to the Khilaafat. When negotiations failed, Mansur sent an army which defeated his uncle.

Mansur ruled for twenty one years and during his rule many uprisings against him were suppressed and the areas of Tabaristan and Daylum were brought under the Abbasid Empire. Khazar, an area near the Armenian border, and Kandar, near the Indian

Part Two

border, also became part of the Empire. Mansur also founded the famous city of Baghdad on the banks of the Tigris River.

After the death of Mansur in 139 A.H., his son Muhammad Al-Mahdi succeeded him. Al-Mahdi ruled until 149 A.H. and was succeeded by his eldest son Musa Al-Hadi who passed away suddenly only after a year and a few months.

Haroon Ar-Rasheed

Haroon Ar-Rasheed was the fifth Kalifha in the Abbasid dynasty and he succeeded his brother Al-Hadi. At the time of his ascension, he was twenty two years old and was the governor of the western provinces. Haroon Ar-Rasheed also experienced many revolts against his Khilaafat but suppressed these revolts and brought the empire under control.

Haroon Ar-Rasheed extended the borders of the Islamic empire by conquering Kabul and many Byzantine cities like Konia, Euphesus, Hereclea and Andrasus. His naval forces also conquered the islands of Rhodes and Cyprus.

Haroon Ar-Rasheed set up his eldest son Ameen as the governor of Iraq, his second son Mamun was made governor of Persia and Khurasan and his third son Musta'sim was made the governor of Jazira (upper Mesopotamia). Haroon Ar-Rasheed also drew up a document, which was hung up in the Ka'bah, stipulating that he was to be succeeded by his son Ameen and thereafter by Mamun and Musta'sim.

The Abbasid Dynasty reached its zenith during the rule of Haroon Ar-Rasheed who will always rank with the great sovereigns and rulers of the world. When a revolt broke out in Transoxia, Haroon

Part Two

Ar-Rasheed personally led an army in this campaign. He passed away on the way to Transoxia at a place called Tus.

Muhammad Al-Ameen bin Haroon

Muhammad Al-Ameen was the eldest son of Haroon Ar-Rasheed and his wife Zubeida. Upon the death of his father, he assumed the Khilaafat and declared the document outlining the succession plan null and void. This caused an uproar in Persia because his half-brother Ma'mun had a Persian mother. This resulted in civil war between Persia and Baghdad.

Muhammad Al-Ameen was defeated by Ma'mun's forces. Ma'mun marched to Baghdad conquering all the towns on the way. Baghdad was held under siege for one year. Al-Ameen was killed and beheaded while trying to escape. He was twenty-seven at the time of his death and ruled for only four years.

Ma'mun Ar-Rasheed

Upon the death of Muhammad Al-Ameen, Ma'mun Ar-Rashid was declared the Khalifah. In the initial years of his rule, he faced many uprisings from the Umayyads, the Alids (descendants of Hadhrat Ali radhiyallahu anhu), etc. Finally, after some years, he managed to suppress the revolts in Baghdad, Egypt and Syria.

It is generally accepted that Ma'mun was one of the greatest Abbasid rulers. During his rule, he promoted the study of various arts, philosophy and sciences and also established libraries and observatories. Many scholars in different fields flourished during his rule and Baghdad became a meeting place for scholars from around the world.

Ma'mun was responsible for imprisoning Imam Ahmad bin Hambal (rahmatullahi alayh), who disagreed with Ma'mun's views on the Mu'tazalites (a sect that does not believe in Taqdeer, predestination or life after death).

Ma'mun's rule for approximately twenty years was a glorious one. He passed away in 218 A.H.

Part Two

Decline of the Abbasid Khilaafat

During the first period of the Abbasid rule, the Ummah reached its peak of prosperity and power. During the second period of the Abbasid rule, separatist movements (pro-independence movements) began to flourish which caused weakness and stagnation in the empire. The second period began upon the death of Khalifah Al Waasiq in 232 A.H.

Turkish and Persian nationals were given key posts in the administration by the Khalifah and they took advantage of this by declaring their independence and the Khalifah was reduced to a symbolic figure. Many small states and caliphates sprang up.

Out of the 37 rulers in the Abbasid dynasty, only a handful like Mansur, Haroon ar-Rasheed and Mamun, were capable of running the empire. Some of the rulers were guilty of oppressive policies and a lot of blood was shed during their rule. There was also a lot of disunity and fighting between rival factions. There was hostility between the Arab tribes and also between Arabs and non-Arabs. Due to the great expansion of the Empire, the treasury could not fulfil the economic demands for its upkeep.

The Abbasids ruled for a period of 508 years until the year 656 A.H. The Abbasid rule finally came to an end when Khalifah Musta'sim was overthrown by the Mongol forces under Hulagu. The Mongol forces massacred nearly the entire population of Baghdad. Musta'sim was taken prisoner and killed.

Achievements of the Abbasid Khilaafat

In the five centuries of Abbasid rule, Muslim cities like Baghdad and Damascus became centres of learning of Islamic and secular knowledge. The Abbasids made progress in the fields of many secular subjects such as algebra, astronomy, medicine and many other related scientific fields. Famous scholars like Ibn Sina and Imaam Razi excelled in the study of medicine.

Great strides and progress in the fields of geography, arts, calligraphy and architecture was also made. Trade and commerce also thrived and many markets were set up in the empire that spread through three continents.

Part Two

The Crusades

In the year 1095 C.E., Pope Urban II announced that the Christians should wage a Holy war against the Muslims. This was called the crusades, which was the turning point in relations between Muslims and the Christians of Europe. 150 000 Europeans took up arms to invade and reclaim the holy lands including Jerusalem.

Before the first crusade, the Muslim empire was already on a decline with the Abbasid rulers losing power to the Buwayhids and later to the Seljuks. It was during this chaos that, Pope Urban II decided to invade the Muslim lands. The crusaders conquered Edessa, Antioch and then marched to Jerusalem and laid siege for a month. Finally they entered Jerusalem and massacred thousands of innocent civilians. History bears testimony to the brutality of this invasion. Approximately 10 000 Muslims were killed near Al-Quds.

After the first crusade, many more followed and Jerusalem became established as a Christian kingdom. Some Muslim rulers rose to the defence of Islam and were able to halt the crusaders advancing into Syria. During the third crusade, Salahuddin Ayyubi raised the call of Jihaad in 1187 C.E. and marched to Jerusalem. In the Battle of Hittin, 20 000 Christians were killed and Jerusalem was captured after eighty-eight years of Christian rule.

This defeat of the Christians led to the king of England, King Richard and other European leaders to take up arms against the Muslims. A battle was fought outside Jerusalem and the Christians were defeated and the peace treaty of Ramla was signed in 1192 C.E.

During the sixth crusade, Jerusalem again fell into Christians hands. Fredrick of Germany declared himself the king of Jerusalem and signed a ten year peace treaty with the Sultan of Egypt. Both parties agreed not to invade each other and Fredrick allowed Muslims to practice their religion freely and also to retain their Masjids.

During the eighth crusade, the Muslims regained control of Jerusalem when the Egyptians defeated the Christians who were led by King Louis IX of France. But due to disunity amongst the Muslims and the deteriorating political conditions in the Muslim world, the economy took a negative turn. The Europeans benefited greatly from the Muslim world in terms of Islamic philosophy, literature and art which contributed greatly to the European renaissance (reawakening).

Part Two

Salahuddin Ayyubi

The Ayyubi Dynasty was founded by Salahuddin Yusuf Bin Ayyub. Under the command of Nurrudin Zangi, Salahuddin Ayyubi overthrew the Fatimids and took over the leadership of Egypt. The Ayyubids ruled Egypt and its surrounds for 79 years between 1171 C.E. and 1250 C.E.

During his early campaigns, Salahuddin Ayyubi conquered Yemen parts of Sudan. In 1172 C.E. he also conquered parts of Africa from Barka (Erithrea) to Gabes (Tunisia). Salahuddin Ayyubi also repulsed (fought back) the crusaders when they invaded Egypt.

Salahuddin Ayyubi marched to Syria and captured Damascus. He then marched to Aleppo, which was controlled by the Zangids, but unsuccessfully retreated to Damascus. Salahuddin Ayyubi defeated the Zangids at Hamah and Turkman's wells in Syria. He then signed a peace treaty with the Zangids and was thereafter recognised as king of Egypt and South Syria. The Abbasids also recognised Salahuddin Ayyubi. Later on he also conquered Allepo, North Mesopotamia and parts of Kurdistan.

Salahuddin Ayyubi confronted the crusaders in July 1187 C.E. at Hittin, defeated them and conquered the entire kingdom of Jerusalem. Besides Tyre and Belfort, most of the cities were conquered by Salahuddin Ayyubi. The Christians marched with an army from Tyre and laid siege to the Muslim controlled Akka for two years. The Muslims eventually surrendered to the Christian leader, King Richard of England, who massacred many Muslim prisoners.

Salahuddin Ayyubi's army was defeated at Arsuf and he retreated to Jerusalem. Richard's army followed Salahuddin Ayyubi to Jerusalem but returned due to internal problems in his (Richard's) army. Richard's army then retreated to Akka. Salahuddin Ayyubi's army followed Richard's army to Akka. Due to Richard's failing health, he signed the peace treaty of Ramla in 1192 C.E. ensuring that Jerusalem remain in Muslim hands but allowed the Christians the right to pilgrimage.

Salahuddin Ayyubi was considered as one of the greatest men of the twelfth century. He was strong, intelligent and pious, and spent most of his life in the best interest of his nation. He built many roads, irrigation canals, Masjids, palaces and forts, and also founded the Ayyubid University in Damascus. Salahuddin Ayyubi ruled for a period of twenty-three years and passed away in Damascus in 1194 C.E. At the time of his death, his rule stretched from the Tigris River in Iraq up to the Nile River in Egypt.

Part Two

Muslim Empires Between the 14ᵗʰ and 19ᵗʰ century

The following five Muslim empires almost simultaneously ruled between the 14ᵗʰ and 19ᵗʰ century.

1. The Ottoman Empire founded by the Turks.
2. The Safavid Empire of Persia (Iran).
3. The Mogul Empire of India.
4. The Mongols of central Asia.
5. Kingdom of Egypt – ruled by various Dynasties.

Only the **Ottoman**, **Mongol** and **Mogul** will be discussed in this book.

Extent of the Ottoman Empire

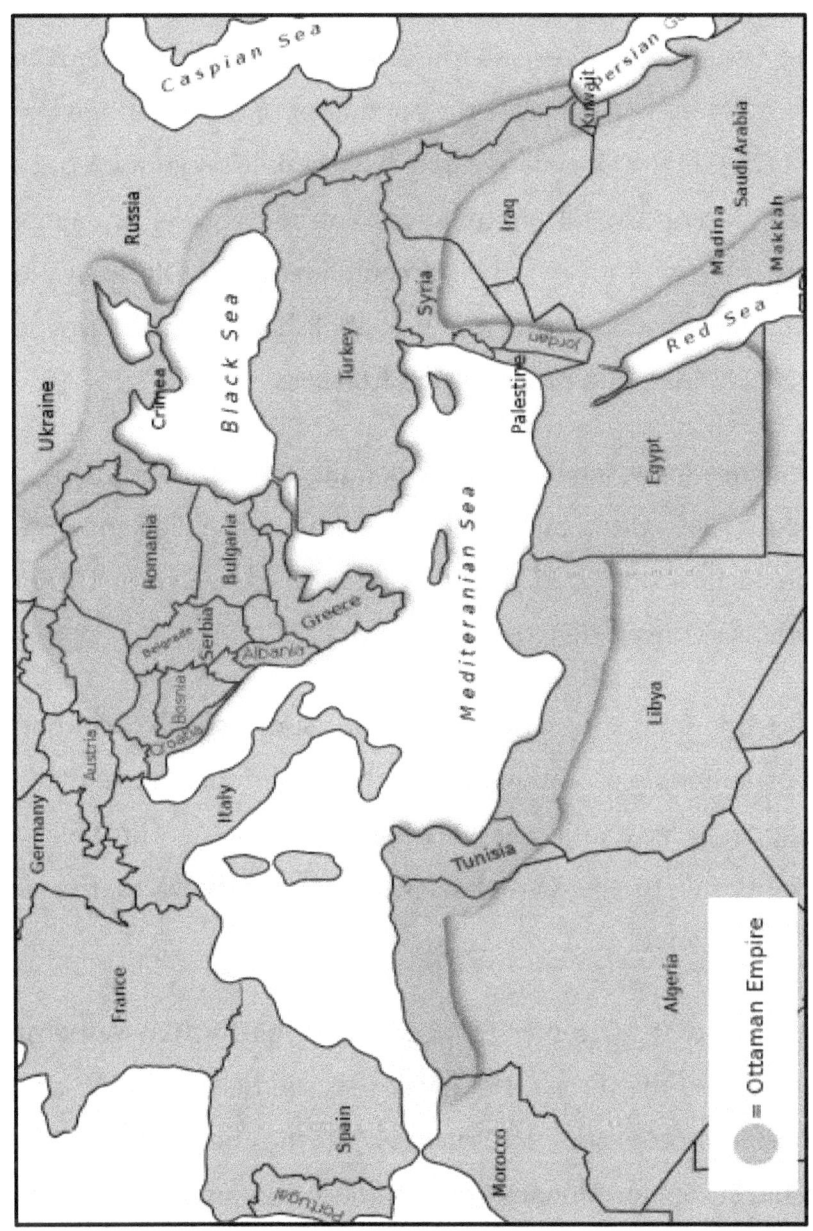

Part Two

The Ottoman Empire - 1200 to 1924 C.E.

The Ottoman Empire was founded by a person called **Uthman**, who defeated Alp Arsalan, the conqueror of the Byzantine Empire; in 1176 C.E. The Ottoman Empire had humble beginnings but soon the Ottoman capital Anatolia (present day Turkey) saw lands on both its east and west being conquered. The Ottoman Empire lasted for over 600 years and was abolished on the 1st November 1924 by **Mustapha Kamal Pasha Ataturk**.

Uthman's grandson, **Suleiman**, conquered Basra and made it his capital. The Ottomans then moved into the Balkans (Greece, Romania, Albania, part of Turkey, etc.) which led to many Roman Catholics converting to Islam.

In 1453 C.E., the Ottomans were successful in conquering Constantinople (Istanbul) making this one of their most important conquest. Constantinople was the centre of the Christian world and its fall to the Ottomans was a major blow to the entire Christian world.

The peak of the Ottoman Empire began when **Sultan Muhammad II** ascended the throne. He developed and beautified the cities of Constantinople and Jerusalem with the help of Sinaan the architect. Sultan Muhammad II turned the famous **Sofia church** into a masjid. The largest masjid, the **Suleiman masjid**, was also built.

Sultan Muhammad II expanded the Empire by conquering Belgrade, Serbia and Bosnia. His attempts at conquering the island of Rhodes, off Greece, were unsuccessful. Mesopotamia and almost all of Arabia was conquered in 1538 C.E. and North Africa was conquered in 1574 C.E.

Sultan Suleiman ruled between 1520 C.E. and 1566 C.E. During his rule, the Ottoman Empire stretched from Vienna, the capital of Austria, to Asia in the east and from North Africa to the Persian Gulf. Hungary also came under Muslim rule in 1526 C.E. which in turn led to many Romanians also accepting Islam. The Ottomans also spread Islam in the Balkans (Greece, Romania, Bulgaria, Serbia, Croatia, etc.).

The final expansion in the Ottoman Empire came with the island of Crete being conquered. Thereafter, the Ottoman power gradually decreased with the death of Sultan Suleiman. Suleiman's successors **Salim II** and **Murad II** were not military strategists and this led to many uprisings and as a result; a decline in the Ottoman Empire. By the 18th century, the Russians and Austrians had taken back the areas around the Caspian Sea. In 1805, the Turkish governor of Egypt, Muhammad Ali, declared Egypt independent of

Part Two

the Ottomans. Greece was lost in the 1820 revolts and Romania gained independence in 1856.

The growing naval power of the west caused the decline of the Ottoman economy. Napoleon of France attacked Egypt between the years 1799 to 1801, but the British defeated Napoleon and forced the French out of Egypt to expand their own colonial interests.

Revolts in Greece in 1820, Serbia and Montenegro in 1920, the Balkan revolt in 1877, Austrian occupation of Bosnia and Herzegovina and the Crimean war with Russia proved impossible to manage and became a strain on the Ottoman Empire's resources. Russia wanted religious powers over the entire Ottoman Empire's Christian subjects. The Ottomans found it difficult to control the religious minorities and the non-Muslim communities. The administration regarded each community as a 'millat' (nation) and gave it the liberty to administer its own affairs according to its own faith, culture and customs.

When the Ottomans refused to accept Christianity, the European powers planned to politically divide the Ottoman Empire, thus causing its downfall and demise. In 1774 under the terms of the **Treaty of Kucuk Kaynarca**, the Christians came under the protection of the Czar (ruler of Russia). In 1856, the treaty of Paris gave the European powers France, Italy and Austria collective authority for the protection of Catholics. Britain, Germany and U.S.A. assumed responsibility for the Protestants. Russia took it upon itself to protect the Orthodox Christians.

In addition to the religious divisions, a number of revolts within the Ottoman Empire were unfolding. The revolts in the Balkans, in Arabia, the Druze in Lebanon, the Armenian rebellion and Egypt being made a British protectorate in 1875 further caused the weakening of the Ottoman Empire.

In 1908, the Young Turk revolution organised by a group of young Turks, **educated and instigated from abroad**, deposed the last strong **Sultan Abdul Hamid**. They demanded a new constitution. In 1914, the Ottoman government was now ruled by three members of the Young Turk Committee. This committee signed a treaty of alliance with Germany on 2 August thereby bringing Turkey into World War 1. Turkey now faced the allied forces on many fronts; the Russian front, the Iraqi front, the Palestinian front, the Egyptian front along the Suez Canal and the Gallipoli front (European sector of Turkey).

The Arabian front:

In 1915, the governor of Egypt, McMahon signed an agreement with Sharif Husain of central Arabia. The **McMahon-Husain**

Part Two

Agreement promised the Arabs independence from Ottoman rule. But the result of this agreement was that the Arab states only got a change of masters.

In 1916, the allies used **Sharif Husain** to spur the Arab tribes to rebel against Turkish rule. The Turkish army was attacked at Madinah and was ousted. Sharif Husain declared himself as King of Arabia. A large chunk of the Ottoman Empire was cut off. Only the province of Hejaz was given to Sharif Husain and the rest of the Arab areas were divided between France and England.

The second agreement in 1916 was that of the **Sykes-Picot Agreement** which planned to divide the entire Middle East into protectorates (areas ruled by the local people but controlled by colonial powers) which would be under French and British influence, until they were strong enough to obtain independence. The French stepped into Syria and Lebanon and the British took over Kuwait, Iraq, Jordan and Palestine. Sharif Husain was left with the province of Hejaz only.

The Palestinian front:

In **The Balfour Declaration** of 1917, the British promised the Jews an independent homeland. This homeland was created out of the Ottoman state of Palestine. A large number of Jews were allowed to migrate from different parts of the world and settle in **Palestine**

which they regarded as the 'Promised Land'. In 1948, Palestine was given to the Jews and the state of Israel came into being with the help of the allied powers. Palestine was divided into three parts- Israel for the Jews, a part for the Palestinian Arabs and Transjordan (over the Jordan River) which was later called Jordan.

During the reign of Sultan Salim I, the Turks had conquered Jerusalem. The Christians were allowed to buy land and settle in Jerusalem. During the First World War, the keys of Jerusalem were obtained by General Allenby of the allied forces and he entered Jerusalem on the 10th December 1917. The Turks vacated Jerusalem on the nights of the 18th and 19th December 1917 without any resIstance. This occupation was regarded as a Christmas gift to the Christians. This occupation was regarded as the end of the First World War and the allied forces declared it as a successful end to a thousand years of Crusader wars.

In 1921, the allied forces - the British, French, Italians and Greeks - invaded Turkey and planned to divide it amongst themselves. The allies made secret pacts rewarding themselves for their successes in the First World War (1914 - 1918). On 1st November 1922, the Sultanate was abolished by Mustafa Kamal bringing an end to 643 years of Ottoman rule. The allies withdrew from Turkey on the 2nd October 1923 and Turkey was declared a republic on the 29th October 1923. On 3rd March 1924, the Khilaafat was abolished.

Part Two

Mustafa Kamal (known as Ata-Turk) declared Turkey a secular state. He adopted the Latin script and **abolished hijab, polygamy and Muslim law**. The European criminal and civil law system was adopted and the country was modernised on European values and ideas. This was the end of the once **Great Ottoman empire**.

Part Two

The Mongols
1206 C.E. - 1370 C.E. (164 years)

Genghis (Changhez) Khan (1206 - 1227 C.E.)

There is no event in the history of Islam that can be compared for its savagery and terror as the Mongol conquest. In the 7th century A.H., 1207 C.E. Genghis (Changhez) Khan united the Mongol tribes with other tribes and invaded many lands including the Islamic Empire. His successors also expanded their power and reign. They conquered land from the shores of China right up to Europe. During their conquests, those who opposed the Mongols were slaughtered and hacked to pieces and their properties were burnt and looted.

Hulagu Khan

Genghis Khan was succeeded by his son Ogadie in 1227 C.E. The next important figure was his grandson, Hulagu Khan, who planned to attack Baghdad, the capital of the Islamic Empire. His army was doubled in number when he was assisted by Christian Georgia. Hulagu's task was made easier as Musta'sim (the 37th and last Abbasid ruler) was but a symbolic ruler, with affairs of the caliphate and real power resting with his officers around him.

Part Two

Musta'sim confronted the forces of Hulagu but was overwhelmed and more than eight 800 000 people were killed. The Mongol forces massacred nearly the entire population of Baghdad. Musta'sim was taken prisoner and killed. For six days and nights the massacre continued and blood flowed like a river.

The fate of Baghdad had shaken everyone who had come to know about it. So many books and manuscripts were thrown into the Tigris River that the heaps almost made a bridge to walk over. Over 500 years of literary works was destroyed. Many schools, libraries and Masjids were burnt.

Thereafter Hulagu established a base in Syria and sent a message to the ruling class (The Mamluks) in Egypt to surrender. But due to the death of Hulagu's brother, Mangu, and succession disputes amongst the Mongols, the Egyptians defeated the Mongols in Syria. In the decisive battle of Ain-Jalut in 1260 C.E., the Mongol army was surrounded and totally defeated.

The battle of Ain-Jalut ended the Mongol dream of expansion and saved Cairo from the fate suffered by the people of Baghdad. It saved the Islamic Empire from complete destruction and dashed the hopes of the Christian world to defeat the Muslims with the assistance of the Mongols. Egypt and Syria were united and the Mamluks tried to revive the Khilaafat.

Part Two

The Mongols accept Islam

After the death of Hulagu in 1265 C.E., Berke Khan succeeded him. Berke Khan and his officers accepted Islam. Even those princes who had taken part in the conquest of Baghdad had secretly accepted Islam. In the year 694 A.H. Kazan, the great grandson of Gengis Khan, accepted Islam publicly whilst sitting on his throne. With him all the Tartars became Muslim. Gold, silver and pearls were given in charity on the day he accepted Islam. He adopted the name Mahmud and attended the Jumuah (Friday) Salaah. Kazan's brother, Aljeito and his son Abu-Said also accepted Islam. Ananda, the grandson of Qublai Khan also accepted Islam. Islam spread in Bukhara, Samarkand and the Golden Horde (north western part of the Mongol Empire extending from Eastern Europe to Siberia).

Many temples were destroyed and non-Muslims were promised protection and in return they had to pay Jizya. Properties that were previously confiscated were returned to their rightful owners and justice was meted out. Islam thus began to emerge out of the ruins of its former glory and once again took up its place as a dominant religion. But within 200 years, the Mongols lost their hold on power in most of the territories and had to return to Mongolia.

Map showing the extent of The Mogul Empire

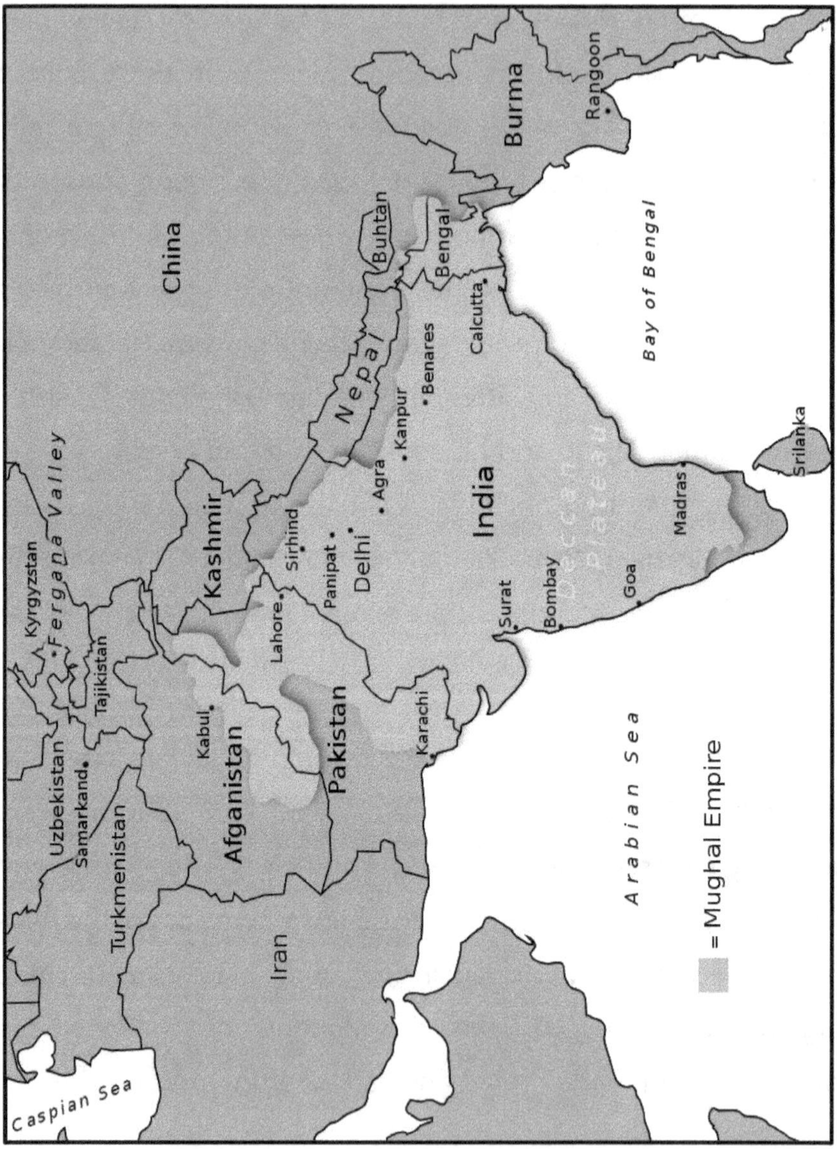

Part Two

The Mogul Empire of India
1526 to 1857 C.E.

NO	RULERS	PERIOD	PERIOD OF RULE
1	Babur	1526 to 1530	4 Years
2	Humayun	1530 to 1556	26 Years
3	Akbar	1556 to 1605	49 Years
4	Jahangir	1605 to 1627	22 Years
5	Shah Jahan	1628 to 1658	30 Years
6	Aurangzeb	1658 to 1707	49 Years
	A number of other rulers followed	To 1857	

Babur

Babur, the founder of the Mogul Dynasty, came from Samarkand and Fergana in Uzbekistan. Babur's father was the prince of Fergana. After his father's death, he was ousted from Fergana and left with his army. He conquered Kabul in 1504 C.E., Lahore in 1526 C.E. and became prince of Kabul.

In the Battle of Panipat, in 1526 C.E., he defeated Ibrahim Lodi and extended his power to Delhi and Agra. Babur established the most glorious empire in India's history and ruled India for just less than four years.

Humayun

Babur was succeeded by his son Humayun who ruled from 1530 C.E. to 1540 C.E. His rule was plagued with misfortune. He was defeated by the Afghan leader Sher Shah and thereafter went into exile for 15 years. He recaptured his empire from Sher Shah in 1555 C.E. and only lived a year after his victory.

Akbar

After Humayun's death, his son Akbar, who was thirteen years of age, was made the king. Akbar's conquests and extensions to the empire were regarded to be the best compared to the other Mogul rulers. His empire extended from Kashmir in the north to the sea shores in the south and Bengal in the east. His system of administration that he introduced forms the basis of present day administration in India.

Akbar ruled justly and tried to forge peace with all the people in the empire. To achieve this goal, he had to develop good relationships with the Hindus and the Rajputs. During the reign of Akbar, a new religious idea, which will have something in common with all the religions, was introduced. He wanted to unite the people on one platform but in the process the Muslims were persecuted and Akbar, who was illiterate, took counsel from the Hindus and the Christians.

Akbar's new religious philosophy was called **'Din-e-Ilahi'**. This new belief system required people to make sajdah (prostrate) to him. He prohibited the killing of cows, celebrated Hindu holy days and worshipped the sun with his Hindu wives. The name Muhammad was not allowed and speaking Arabic was a crime. Muslims were also prevented from going for Haj.

Akbar issued a 'royal infallibility' decree that he was guarded from making any error and all his opinions had to be observed by the Muslims. Three years later, Akbar declared **'Din-e-Ilahi'** to be the official religion of the state. But this decree was vigorously opposed from all parts of India and was hardly ever practised outside the royal court. **Hadhrat Mujaddid Alf-Thani (rahmatullahi alayh)** was amongst the leading Ulama who opposed Akbar openly.

The non-Muslims used this opportunity to spread their corrupt ways. There was a decline in moral behaviour and people began celebrating other religious festivals. People also began to deal in interest openly. Akbar abolished Jizya and blended Hindu and

Part Two

Muslim style and design in palace architecture, literature and music. As a result of Akbar's policies, Islamic education suffered to a great extent.

Marriages with Hindu and Rajput women served to weaken the cause of Islam and brought about interference in government policies. The women Akbar married kept to their own faith and worship practices. These marriages which were un-Islamic and unlawful, eventually led to cruel family feuds.

Although Akbar built a mighty empire, his enthusiasm to appease the non-Muslims for paltry political gain compromised Islam. His introducing innovations and kufr beliefs was instrumental in weakening the cause and influence of Deen. Akbar died at the age of 62. His rule lasted 49 years.

Jahangir

Akbar was succeeded by his son Jahangir, who was 37 years old at the time of his ascension. Jahangir abolished all innovations and kufr beliefs and policies of his late father. This was not liked by the Hindus and they incited his son Khurso to rise up against his father. Initially he had some success but was finally defeated.

In 1615 C.E. Jahangir entered into a commercial treaty with the British, which allowed the British concessions, but two and half

Centuries later, in 1858, led to the overthrow of the Mogul Empire. Jahangir died in 1627 C.E. after 27 years of rule.

During this difficult period for Islam emerged **Shaikh Ahmed Sirhindi** (rahmatullahi alayh), a great reformer who was popularly known as **Mujaddid Alf-Saani**. He was born in 1562 C.E. when Akbar's misguided beliefs were being preached. It was due to the efforts of Shaikh Ahmed Sirhindi (rahmatullahi alayh) that Akbar's 'Din-e-Ilahi' was not able to take root and flourish.

Amongst some of his writings was "Proof of Prophethood" and "Fighting the Rejectors". Shaikh Ahmed Sirhindi (rahmatullahi alayh) called people to the truth and established the Sunnah. He enjoyed popular support from the people and many came from far and wide to benefit from him. Jahangir once ordered him to appear in his court. When Shaikh Ahmed Sirhindi (rahmatullahi alayh) arrived, he did not prostate before the king. This angered the king and Shaikh Ahmed Sirhindi (rahmatullahi alayh) was imprisoned. Many Hindus converted to Islam when the Shaikh was in prison. The king released him and apologised.

Shaikh Ahmed Sirhindi (rahmatullahi alayh) wrote to the princes of the region inviting them to Islam. He once wrote; **"It is hard for every Muslim to see that the rituals of the non-Muslims are still being practiced and preserved. Muslims must put an end to**

Part Two

this behaviour." Not only did he tirelessly attack the deviant beliefs but also the preaching of corrupt scholars and the misguided Sufis. Shaikh Ahmed Sirhindi (rahmatullahi alayh) passed away in 1642 C.E. and is buried in Sirhind.

Shah Jahan

Prince Khurram, popularly known as Shah Jahan, succeeded Jahangir in February 1628 C.E. Shah Jahan promised Shaikh Ahmed Sirhindi (rahmatullahi alayh) that he would do away with the deviant beliefs his grandfather had introduced but no significant progress was made in this regard.

In 1631 C.E. Shah Jahan's wife, who bore him 14 children, passed away. To commemorate her death he built the famous Taj Mahal over her tomb in Agra. The building took approximately 17 years to build between 1631 C.E. and 1648 C.E.

During his reign, Shah Jahan faced many revolts and also undertook many expeditions. In 1652 C.E. he defeated the Portuguese at Hugli and it was brought under Muslim rule. He also undertook campaigns to the Deccan, Kamrup, Persia and central Asia all of which helped in extending the borders of the empire. Shah Jahan fell ill in 1658 C.E. and eventually passed away in 1666 C.E.

Part Two

Aurangzeb (Aalamgeer)

When Shah Jahan fell ill in 1658 C.E., his four sons began a power struggle for the throne. The favourite son of Shah Jahan named Dara Shiku first assumed power. His brother Shuja, who was the viceroy of Bengal, marched with his forces to face Dara Shiku but was unsuccessful. Two other brothers Aurangzeb and Murad, the viceroys of Deccan and Gujarat respectively, joined forces against Dara. Dara was defeated in battle and Aurangzeb ascended the throne in July 1658 C.E.

Even after his ascension, Aurangzeb's brothers still tried to take control of the empire by force. Dara Shiku's army faced Aurangzeb in Punjab. Dara Shiku was taken captive in 1659 C.E. and executed on charges of apostasy. Shuja's army was defeated by Aurangzeb at Khawaja in 1659 C.E. and Shuja was assassinated after this battle. Murad was in prison for three years and then tried for murder and executed in 1661 C.E. Aurangzeb became the undisputed leader of the Mogul Empire after the death of his three brothers. Most of the Indian Sub-continent came under his rule, from Kabul to Agra and from the Himalayas to the southern shores.

Aurangzeb suppressed revolts by the Marathas in the 1660's and the Pathans in the 1670's. Aurangzeb's reign saw the recovery of Islam. He did away with all un-Islamic laws, treated the Ulama with

Part Two

great respect and cancelled many unjust taxes. He prohibited singing and music in the palaces. He built new Masaajid, renovated existing ones and also saw to the effort of Dawah towards Islam.

One of the most remarkable achievements of Aurangzeb was the compilation of the **"Fatawa Alamghiri"** by various Ulama. This compilation was an Islamic reference, setting out the views of the Hanafi Ulama. Aurangzeb taught the Qur'aan to those Hindus who had accepted Islam.

Aurangzeb was ninety years of age when he passed away. The cloth to shroud him cost a mere five Rupees which was paid from the money he earned in making and selling hats. He ruled India for fifty years. May Allah Ta'ala grant him Jannah.

On the death of Aurangzeb, his three sons fought to succeed him. Shah Alam, who assumed the title "Bahadur Shah Zafar I", succeeded his father Aurangzeb. Bahadur Shah Zafar I was 70 years old when he ascended the throne. He was a Shia and tried to make Shiasm the state religion but was stopped by strong public opposition. Bahadur Shah Zafar I died in 1712 and was succeeded by his son Jahandar who only ruled for less than a year.

Jahandar's nephew Farouk Siyyer overthrew him and became the next emperor of Delhi. After being cured of a deadly disease by a British surgeon, the British were granted many concessions which gave rise to British political power. Farouk Siyyer ruled for six years. After his death, anarchy set in and a number of rulers followed and the once mighty Mogul rulers were now a weakened force.

The fall of the Mogul empire

The Mogul Empire came to an end after 332 years of rule from 1526 C.E. to 1858 C.E. During the first two Centuries, the Moguls rose to great heights becoming one of the leading world powers but thereafter lost their country to the British who initially came as traders but stripped the Moguls of all power.

Bahadur Shah Zafar II was the last Mogul ruler. He was stripped of all power by the British and became a figurehead around whom the people of Delhi tried to rally during the 1857 mutiny against the British. The mutiny was not successful and the British regained power. Bahadur Shah Zafar II, in his old age, was kept a prisoner and his two sons were shot and beheaded by General Hudson in front of a crowd of Hindus. Bahadur Shah Zafar II was overthrown and removed by the British and exiled to the Burmese capital Rangoon. Not only did the Mogul rule come to an end but also a thousand years of Muslim rule which was a great blow for Islam.

Some of the Mogul leaders caused harm to Islam by introducing innovations and kufr beliefs and dawah was neglected. It was the

Part Two

Sufi and Aulia-Allah who carried the propagation and spread of Islam assisted by leaders like Aurangzeb. When all sorts of evil and corruption crept into the Mogul rule, then this was their downfall. The downfall of the Abbasid rule followed a similar pattern.

These mistakes of evil and corruption continue in the so called Islamic countries of today. The only solution is the implementation of the Qur'aan and Sunnah of Rasulullah ﷺ by all leaders and common people alike.

Part Three

PART THREE

The importance of Taqleed and a brief History of the four Imaams

Before outlining the lives of the four great Imams, one has to understand why there is a need to follow them. Below is a brief account why we follow the four great Imaams in matters pertaining to our daily lives.

Submitting oneself to the commands of Allah Ta'ala as shown to mankind by Ambiyaa (alayhimus salaam);

The reason for the creation of mankind by Allah Ta'ala is that man is required to pledge total obedience to Allah Ta'ala and to worship Him alone. It was for this reason that Allah Ta'ala sent down a chain of Ambiyaa (alayhimus salaam) who were his vicegerents on earth, sent to guide man towards the commandments of Allah Ta'ala and how to worship the one and only Allah Ta'ala. Therefore man was supposed to follow Ambiyaa (alayhimus salaam) totally in all respects. Allah Ta'ala mentions in the Qur'aan

He who obeys the messenger [Nabi ﷺ] has indeed obeyed Allah. (Surah nisaa: Ayat 80)

Part Three

After the demise of Rasulullah ﷺ, people used **"to follow"** the learned Sahaabah (radhiyallahu anhum).

Definition and the importance of Taqleed;

The literal meaning of taqleed is **"to follow"**. The Shar'i definition is to subject oneself totally and accept the opinions of the experts in Qur'aan and Hadith. Like how we submit ourselves to the opinions of the experts regarding our worldly affairs (e.g. Doctors, lawyers, economists, etc.), likewise regarding our Deeni affairs we should submit ourselves to the experts who are proficient and educated in this field.

The inception of Taqleed goes back to the time of Sahaabah (radhiyallahu anhum). From the time of Rasulullah ﷺ, there were those Sahaabah (radhiyallahu anhum) like Abdullah bin Masood (radhiyallahu anhu), Muaaz bin Jabal (radhiyallahu anhu), etc. who were famous for their in-depth Islamic knowledge. After the demise of Rasulullah ﷺ, many of the Sahaabah (radhiyallahu anhum) migrated to different lands, and became the Imaams and leaders in those lands guiding the masses in Deeni matters. The general people actually made Taqleed of those Sahaabah (radhiyallahu anhum) by following them. Some of the Sahaabah (radhiyallahu anhum) who were regarded as Imaams in different countries, towns, etc. are listed below;

Part Three

1. Abdullah bin Abbaas رضي الله عنه - Makkah
2. Zaid bin Saabit رضي الله عنه - Madinah
3. Abdullah bin Masood رضي الله عنه - Kufa
4. Muaaz bin Jabal رضي الله عنه - Yemen
5. Anas bin Maalik رضي الله عنه - Basra

Making Taqleed continued in the era of the Tabieen (those people who saw the Sahaabah (radhiyallahu anhum). Some of the famous learned experts in Deen amongst the Tabieen were;

1. Nafi (rahmatullahi alayh) - Madinah
2. Ataa (rahmatullahi alayh) - Makkah
3. Yahya bin Katheer (rahmatullahi alayh) - Yamamah
4. Mak'hool (rahmatullahi alayh) - Syria
5. Hasan Basri (rahmatullahi alayh) - Basra
6. Ibrahim Nakh'ee (rahmatullahi alayh) - Kufa

In every major town, certain Imaams used to pass a ruling which was followed by the general masses. Initially, there were many Imaams and Mazaahib (plural of mazhab), but as time passed, all the Mazaahib ceased to exist after the demise of their Imaams and the four famous Mazaahib viz. Hanafi, Maaliki, Shafi'ee and Hambali were established and remain to this day.

Part Three

Some of the reasons given for the continuity of only the four Mazaahib are as follows;

1. The four Imaams were more famous and accepted by majority of the people.
2. Compared to the other Imaams, the four Imaams attracted students in large numbers.
3. After the demise of other Imaams, many people turned to these four Imaams.
4. These four Mazaahib had made a concerted effort to have recorded every facet of a Muslim's life, whereas this was not the same for the other Mazaahib.

Why follow one Imaam only?

Allah Ta'ala says in the Qur'aan; "And do not follow your desires, for it will mislead you from the path of Allah." (Surah Sad Ayat 26)

Although all four Mazaahib are correct, one should adhere to only one mazhab and not change from mazhab to mazhab as this will amount to following one's own desires. If a person will not follow one Imaam, then he will always see which mazhab provides an easy solution and this will lead him to follow his own desires and passions. The four great Imaams were no ordinary people, and as such, set an extremely high standard in their personal adherence to Deen as well as interpreting Qur'aan and Hadith for the people

Part Three

who were to come after them. Therefore, it is important that we follow only one single Imaam. Below is a brief life sketch of each Imaam.

Lessons:

1. Always keep contact with your Utaads, Ulama and pious seniors.
2. Stick to what you learnt under your Ustaaz in madrasah.
3. Any questions and doubts should be referred to your Ustaaz and righteous Ulama. They will always be glad to help you.
4. **Stick to one particular mazhab** as this will protect you from following your desires.

Part Three

Brief life sketches of the four Imaams from whom the four mazhabs originated

NO	IMAAMS	BORN	DIED	AGE
1	Imaam Abu Hanifa رحمةالله	80 A.H.	150 A.H.	70
2	Imaam Maalik رحمةالله	93 A.H.	179 A.H.	86
3	Imaam Shaafi رحمةالله	150 A.H.	204 A.H.	54
4	Imaam Ahmad bin Hambal رحمةالله	164 A.H.	241 A.H.	77

Imaam Abu Hanifa رحمةالله

Imaam Abu Hanifa's (rahmatullahi alayh) actual name was Nu'maan bin Saabit. His father spent his childhood in the service of Hadhrat Ali (radhiyallahu anhu). Imaam Abu Hanifa (rahmatullahi alayh) was born in 80 A.H. in the famous city of Kufa in Iraq, during the Umayyad rule of Abdul Malik bin Marwaan. He was a cloth merchant by trade and his shop was situated close to the Jaamia Masjid in Kufa. Despite being a wealthy person, Imaam Abu Hanifa (rahmatullahi alayh) was never wasteful and his monthly expenses did not exceed two Dirhams.

Many Sahaabah and Taabieen used to reside in Kufa, which was a hub of Knowledge. Imaam Sha'bee (rahmatullahi alayh), a great scholar, encouraged Imaam Abu Hanifa (rahmatullahi alayh) to

Part Three

acquire knowledge by telling him, "I see signs of intelligence in you. You ought to sit in the company of the learned." This spurred his quest for knowledge. At the age of twenty-two, Imaam Abu Hanifa (rahmatullahi alayh) travelled to Makkah, Madinah, Basra, etc, in pursuit of knowledge. He studied under many learned and expert teachers. Imaam Abu Hanifa (rahmatullahi alayh) probably studied under all the scholars of Hadith of the time in Kufa.

Imaam Abu Hanifa (rahmatullahi alayh) was the first person to have codified and categorized Islamic Fiqh (jurisprudence). It was for this reason that Imaam Shaafi (rahmatullahi alayh) used to say; "People are indebted to Imaam Abu Hanifa (rahmatullahi alayh) in fiqh." The Hanafi mazhab is not solely based on the views and opinions of Imaam Abu Hanifa (rahmatullahi alayh) only, but rather it is a school of thought formulated by the Imaam and more than forty of his dedicated students who themselves were experts in the various branches of Deen. Imaam Abu Hanifa (rahmatullahi alayh) also authored many books. Imaam Shaafi (rahmatullahi alayh) said; "The person who has not studied the books of Imaam Abu Hanifa (rahmatullahi alayh) cannot become proficient in fiqh."

Amongst the many qualities found in Imaam Abu Hanifa (rahmatullahi alayh) was his high degree of tolerance, patience, independent thought, quick wittedness, generosity and piety. For forty years, he read Esha and Fajr Salaah with the same wudhu.

Part Three

Imaam Abu Hanifa (rahmatullahi alayh) once refused the position of being a judge, for which he was imprisoned in Baghdad by the Abbasid Khalifah, Abu Ja'far Mansur, and flogged a hundred and ten lashes. Thereafter he was poisoned and he finally passed away while in sajdah in Rajab 150 A.H. and was buried in Baghdad. About 50 000 people attended his janazah.

Part Three

Imaam Maalik رَحْمَةُٱللَّهِ

Imaam Maalik (rahmatullahi alayh) was born in 93 A.H. in Madinah Munawwarah, in a pious family who were well-known for their knowledge. He memorised the Qur'aan Shareef in his early childhood and then began to study and memorise Hadith. At the tender age of seventeen, he began teaching Hadith. He compiled a book on Hadith called "Mu'atta" which was one of the first books of Hadith on fiqh (jurisprudence) and took eleven years to compile. Amongst his illustrious students are Imaam Shaafi (rahmatullahi alayh), Imaam Muhammad (rahmatullahi alayh) and Abdullah bin Mubaarak (rahmatullahi alayh).

Imaam Maalik (rahmatullahi alayh) was famous for his piety and he strongly adhered to the Sunnah. On one occasion he was conducting Hadith lessons when his face changed colour. On enquiry, the students were told that he was bitten by a scorpion thirteen times but due to respect for Hadith he did not stop the lesson. He never rode an animal in Madinah saying: "I feel ashamed to ride an animal on the soil where Rasulullah ﷺ placed his feet."

Imaam Maalik (rahmatullahi alayh) passed away at the age of eighty-six in Rabiul Awwal 179 A.H. in Madinah and was buried in the cemetery of Baqee.

Part Three

Imaam Shafi'ee رَحْمَةُٱللَّهِ

Imaam Shafi'ee (rahmatullahi alayh) was born in 150 A.H. in a place called Asqalaan near Baitul Maqdis in Palestine. In the same year that Imaam Shafi'ee (rahmatullahi alayh) was born, Imaam Abu Hanifa (rahmatullahi alayh) passed away.

Imaam Shafi'ee (rahmatullahi alayh) began his quest for knowledge in his childhood. He completed the hifz of Qur'aan at the age of nine. At the age of thirteen, he gained expertise in Arabic grammar, literature and poetry. He also began seeking knowledge in Hadith and Fiqh (jurisprudence) from the scholars of Makkah. At the age of fourteen, he was given permission to issue fatwa (Islamic verdict or decree). He also travelled to Madinah Munawarah and studied the "Mu'atta" under Imaam Maalik (rahmatullahi alayh) and memorised it in eight months. He later on migrated to Egypt. Some scholars say that Imaam Shafi'ee (rahmatullahi alayh) was the first person to write a book on Usoolul Fiqh (principles of Islamic jurisprudence).

Imaam Shafi'ee (rahmatullahi alayh) was famous for his generosity and simplicity. In the month of Ramadhaan, he used to recite the Qur'aan Shareef sixty times in nafl Salaat. Imaam Shafi'ee (rahmatullahi alayh) passed away on a Friday at the age of fifty four in 204 A.H. in Egypt and was buried at the time of Asr Salaah.

Part Three

Imaam Ahmad bin Hambal ﷺ

Imaam Ahmad bin Hambal (rahmatullahi alayh) was born in Rabiul Awwal 164 A.H. in Baghdad. He was of Arab origin, of the Shaibaan clan which is from the noble lineage of Rasulullah ﷺ. He began memorising the Qur'aan Shareef at a very early age in Baghdad. He commenced his studies in Hadith at the age of sixteen. He memorised about a million Ahaadith. Amongst his outstanding students were the likes of Imaam Bukhari (rahmatullahi alayh), Imaam Muslim (rahmatullahi alayh) and Imaam Abu Dawood (rahmatullahi alayh).

Imaam Ahmad (rahmatullahi alayh) always strictly adhered to the Sunnah. His life was one of sincerity, piety and simplicity. Imaam Ahmad (rahmatullahi alayh) used to perform 300 rakaats of nafl Salaah daily.

Imaam Ahmad (rahmatullahi alayh) passed away at the age of seventy seven in Rabiul Awwal 241 A.H. on Friday in Baghdad. Approximately eight hundred thousand (800 000) people attended his Janaaza Salaah.

Part Three

Map of Palestine

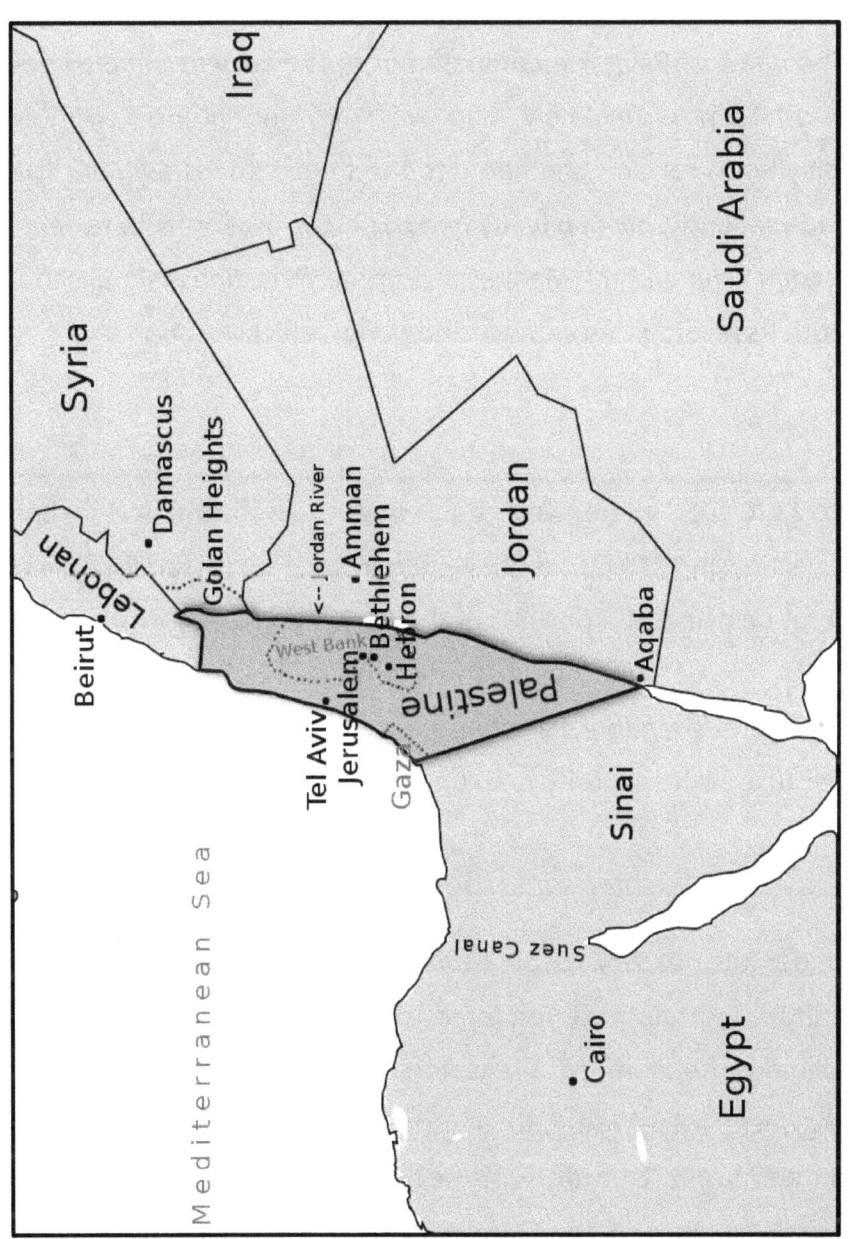

Part Three

Palestine

The name of Palestine originated from the ancient people known as Philistines. This holy land was the land of many Ambiyaa (alayhimus salaam) and home to the three famous religions Islam, Judaism and Christianity. Its geographical location is between the Jordan River and the Mediterranean Sea. Palestine is significant for both its religious importance and geographical location.

Population

In 1170 C.E., there were only 1440 Jews living in the entire Palestine. In 1270 C.E., there were only two Jewish families living in Jerusalem. In 1917, only 9% of the population was Jewish and 91% Arab. The 91% Arab population comprised 80% Muslim and 11% Christians. Therefore, Palestine can be regarded as an Arab country because of the majority Arab population.

Islam in Palestine, the UN mandate and recent events

Under the leadership of Amirul Mumineen Umar (radhiyallahu anhu), Jerusalem surrendered peacefully and he guaranteed religious freedom to all its inhabitants. Besides the 87 years between 1099-1186 C.E. of Christian rule, Palestine remained under Muslim control from the 7th to the 20th century. Palestine was a province of the Ottoman Empire when British forces took command of the region during World War One. The British commander, General Allenby, entered Jerusalem on 11 December 1917, (730 years after Salahuddin Ayyubi conquered Jerusalem).

The League of Nations gave Britain the mandate over Palestine. Britain allowed an influx of Jewish immigrants to swell the number of Jews living in Palestine. When the Arab – Israeli war erupted in 1948, the Arabs comprised 68% and the Jews 32% of the population. Arabs were then expelled from Jewish occupied territory and the Muslims now represent only 18% and the Jews nearly 80%.

The United Nations partition of Palestine in 1947 gave the Jews over 56% of the total land area, which was ten times more than what they owned at the time. The expelled Arab population, totalling more than 4.5 million, are now refugees and scattered all over the world. The majority of the refugees are concentrated in the West Bank (West of the Jordan River), the Gaza strip, Jordan, Lebanon and Syria.

After the war, the League of Nations gave Britain the mandate to prepare the population for self-rule. The British also assisted immigration of Jewish people to Palestine. France and Britain, the colonialist powers in the region, divided the entire Middle East so that it could not be a single forceful power in the region. This was

Part Three

made possible by the **'Sykes and Picot agreement'** signed in 1916. This agreement gave Britain Southern Syria extending to Iraq including Baghdad and Basra and France got Syria and up to Mosul in Iraq.

After this agreement, the leaders of the Zionist movement established contact with the British Government which led to the establishment of the infamous **'Balfour Declaration'** on 2 November 1917. This declaration promised a 'National Home for the Jewish people in Palestine'. This declaration was in direct conflict with the promises of independence that Britain had made to the Arabs.

The Palestinians and some Arab countries raised objections to the declaration. But it became clear that Britain was determined in carrying out its intentions against the wishes of the Arab population. In November 1947, the United Nations General Assembly passed a resolution dividing Palestine into Jewish and Arab areas which was rejected by the Arabs. The resolution granted 56% of the most fertile land to the Jews. The Jews then waged a war of terror against the Arab population.

The British then left the mandated territory and the new state of Israel came into being. This unilateral decision, to create the state of Israel on Palestinian land, was taken on 14 May 1948. The

Part Three

Palestinian people were thus deprived of their homeland and mercilessly uprooted, dispersed and made refugees. Palestine, which was their homeland for over a thousand years, was taken without their consent by force and the state of Israel came into being.

Israel launched two large scale wars against the Palestinians in 1956 and 1967. In June 1967, Israel occupied the Sinai in Egypt up to the Suez Canal, the Golan Heights in Syria and all Palestinian land west of the Jordan River. All appeals by public opinion and United Nations resolutions for withdrawal from the occupied land were ignored by the Israelis. In October 1973 Israel waged yet another war and continues its military aggression, brutality, terrorism, subjugation and subversion against the innocent Palestinian people.

Part Three

The extent of Palestinian land that was occupied over the years by the Jews

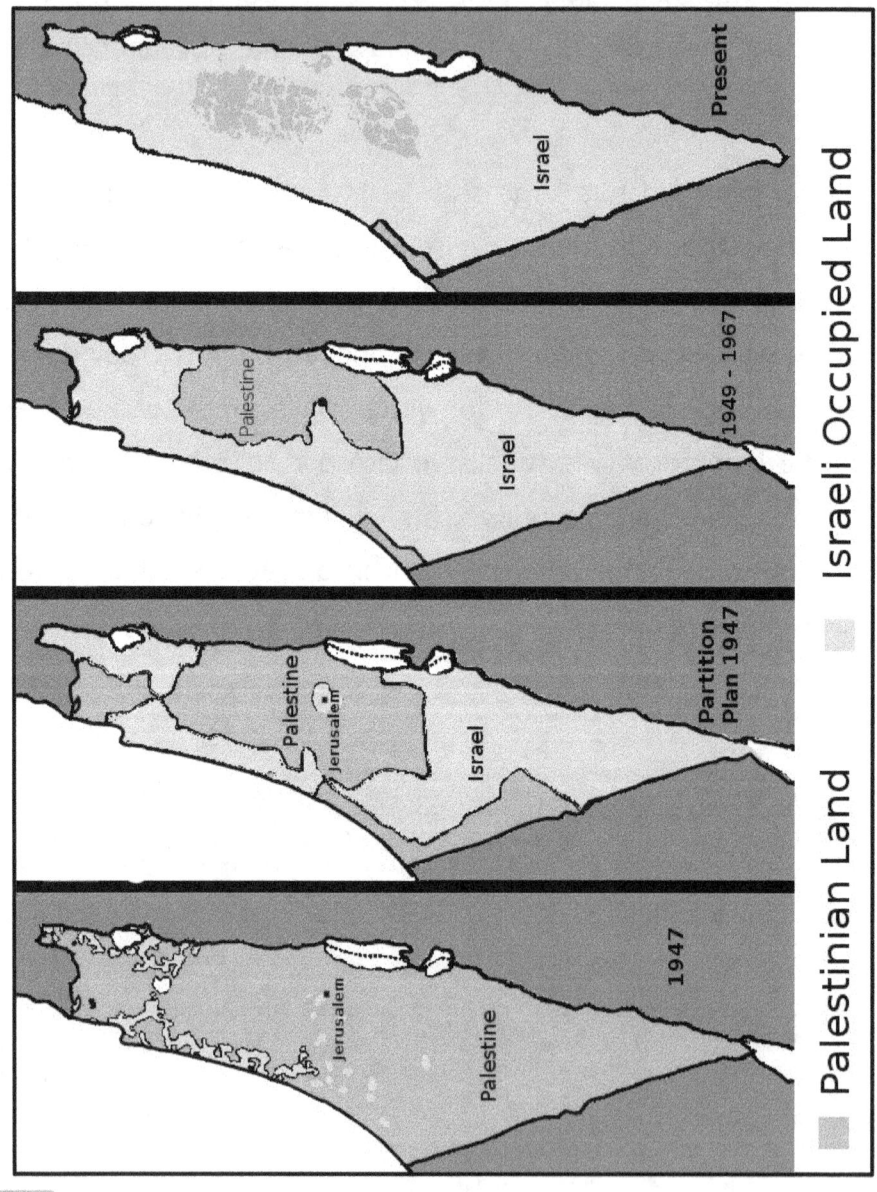

Part Three

Why Palestine is important to the Muslims?

1. It is described in the Qur'aan Shareef as the "Holy Land" and also the "Blessed Land".
2. Masjidul Aqsa is the second oldest place of worship, built by Ebrahim (alayhis salaam) forty years after he built the Ka'bah Shareef in Makkah.
3. Many Ambiyaa (alayhimus salaam) were born and buried in Palestine.
4. Masjidul Aqsa was the first Qiblah of the Muslims.
5. The incident of Miraaj, where Rasulullah's ﷺ miraculous journey to the seven heavens, was from Jerusalem.
6. Many Sahaabah (radhiyallahu anhum) and scholars migrated to Palestine and are buried there.

Part Three

Routes taken to bring Labour and Political Exiles to South Africa

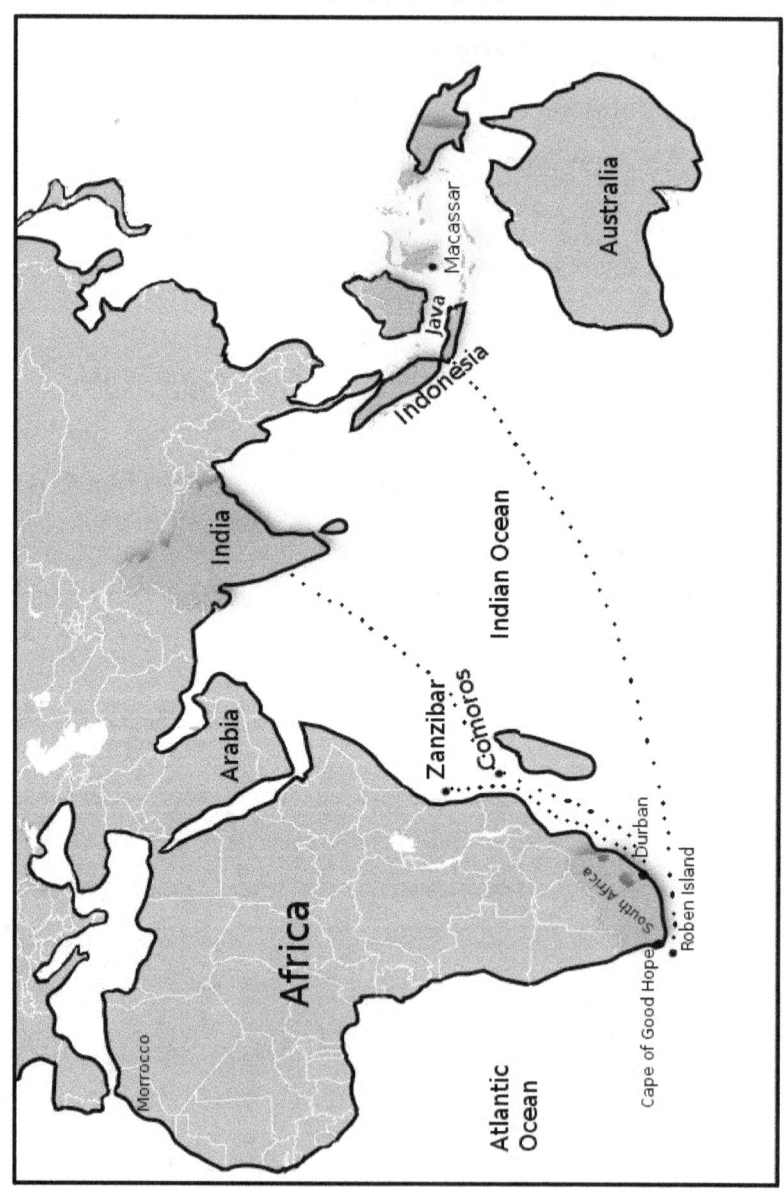

Islam in South Africa

The first known Muslims to arrive at the Cape of Good Hope in South Africa were the Malay people in 1652. Some of them arrived as political prisoners who were banished to hard labour at the Cape of Good Hope. A labour force of free Muslims arrived from Indonesia at the request of Jan Van Riebeeck. However, according to Dutch law, they were not allowed to practice Islam openly. In 1667, more political exiles arrived at the Cape. They were banished from their native lands because they posed a threat to the Dutch.

Shaikh Yusuf

The most famous of the political prisoners, who was exiled to the Cape, was Shaikh Yusuf of Macassar who was a man of noble birth. He was born in 1626. He arrived in South Africa on the 2nd April 1694 along with forty-nine other exiles and his two wives. He was exiled because of his opposition to the colonial rule of the Dutch.

Shaikh Yusuf was welcomed and housed at Zandvleit by Simon van der Stel who was the governor of the Cape. Zandvleit became the first Muslim community in South Africa. Shaikh Yusuf passed away on the 23rd May 1699 at the age of 73 and was buried at Zandvleit in the Cape.

Part Three

The Rajah of Tambora (Abdul Basi Sultana)

Three years after Shaikh Yusuf's arrival in the Cape, Abdul Basi Sultana, the Rajah of Tambora in Indonesia, arrived in the Cape. He arrived in chains in the Cape for opposing Dutch colonial rule in his native Indonesia. Initially, he was kept at the stables at the castle in Cape Town but by the intervention of Shaikh Yusuf, he was allowed to live in isolation at Vergelegen. At Vergelegen he wrote the first Qur'aan in the Cape from memory. This Qur'aan was given to the governor Simon van der Stel.

De Vryezwarten

In 1743, the Dutch brought more Muslim prisoners from Indonesia to the Cape to build a new break-water (pier). After serving their sentences, many prisoners decided to stay and these people were known as the "De Vryezwarten" (The free black community).

Between 1770 and 1800, De Vryezwarten were responsible for the spread of Islam in the colony. By 1800, the number of Muslims living in the Cape rose to over 3000.

Tuang Guru (Abdullah bin Qadhi Abdus Salaam)

Abdullah bin Qadhi Abdus Salaam, commonly known as "Tuang Guru", was a prince in one of the Indonesian Islands. He was born in 1712 and was a son of a Qadhi. His lineage is linked to the Sultan of Morocco and Rasulullah ﷺ.

On 6th April 1780, he was brought as a prisoner to Cape Town and imprisoned on Robben Island. During his imprisonment, he wrote several copies of the Holy Qur'aan from memory. He also wrote a book on Fiqh titled, "Ma'rifatul Islam Wal Imaan". Tuang Guru was released from Robben Island in 1793.

He married a free woman Kaija van de Kaap who bore him two children. He established the first madrasah in a warehouse and converted many slaves to Islam. The madrasah was situated in Dorp Street and had 375 slave children. In 1794, the first Masjid, "Awwal Masjid", was opened in Dorp Street and Tuang Guru was the Imaam. Tuang Guru passed away in 1807, at the age of 95. At the time of his death, his madrasah had approximately 491 students.

By 1840, the Muslim population in Cape Town numbered approximately 6400. Also in 1840, in the city of Port Elizabeth,

Part Three

there were 150 Muslims who built the first Masjid in 1849. Today the Cape Province has a huge Muslim community with many Masjids and madrasahs in most of the towns.

The arrival of Muslims of Indian Origin

Like the Malay Muslims who had arrived in the Cape, the first batch of 342 Indian labourers arrived on 6th November 1860 in Durban aboard the SS Truro. Only 24 were Muslim and out of the 24 only 9 remained after completing their time. Approximately 170 Muslims arrived between the years 1860 and 1861 as labourers from India.

In 1869, Muslim Indians of Gujarati, Urdu, Marathi and Kathiawar backgrounds came to South Africa as free passenger Indians at their own expense with the intention of doing trade. These Muslims were referred to as 'Arabs' so as to distinguish them from their non-Muslim Indian countrymen.

The Muslim Indian community spread into the urban and rural areas of Transvaal, present day Gauteng and Mpumalanga, and established retail and wholesale businesses. Masjids and Makaatib were also established in all regions where the Muslims had settled. In 1870, Johannesburg's first Masjid was initially a tent in Kerk Street and in 1888 a building was constructed. The first Masjid in Durban was built in 1881 in Grey Street.

Part Three

The Makaatib: Wherever the Muslims settled, they established Masaajid and Makaatib for the religious education of their children. This helped with the preservation of the Deen of Islam. This institution of the Maktab, although seemingly insignificant, played an important part in the preservation of the Islamic identity. It protected their beliefs and gave them a basic understanding of Islam.

With the makaatib, the Tablighi Jamaat also made great strides in the preservation of Deen in South Africa. With the Tabligh effort progressing, many people were affected and this spurred people to educate their children as Ulama. Initially higher Islamic education was acquired at Darul Ulooms in India and other countries but subsequently many Darul Ulooms were established on South African soil. These institutions produced many Ulama who serve the Islamic needs of the Muslim population up to this day.

Part Three

Muslims from Zanzibar

In 1873, the province of Natal saw the arrival of Muslims from the Island of Zanzibar. They were brought by the British to work on the sugar cane plantations. The first batch of 113 arrived aboard the HMS Briton on the 4th August 1873. A year later a group of 81 more arrived.

The first Zanzibari community was established in the Kings Rest area in Natal. Here they established a Masjid and Madrasah and brought an Imaam from the Comore Islands. During the apartheid years the Zanzibari community was moved from the Kings Rest area to Chatsworth.

Islamic Organisations in South Africa

Currently, South Africa has a large number of Muslim organisations involved in the propagation of Islam, charitable and social work, schools, makaatib and Darul Ulooms. Amongst the early organisations founded in South Africa are the Jamiatul Ulama Transvaal founded in 1923 and the Waterval Islamic Institute opened in July 1940 by Hajee Moosa Ismail Mia and Moulana Muhammad Mia.

Part Three

Today, South African Muslims have advanced in many sectors of society. In addition to Dawah and Deeni Taleem in South Afrrica and internationally, South African Muslims have also contributed in the fields of medicine, commerce, engineering and a host of other fields. Many businessmen have also prospered in many regions of the country.

With the fall of 'apartheid', the challenges facing the Muslim are ever increasing. Islam is now spreading in the black and white communities in all regions of the country. May Allah Ta'ala guide us and accept us in the upliftment and spreading of His Deen. Aameen.

Lessons:

1. When our forefathers migrated to foreign lands, the first thing that they established was **Masaajid and madrasahs**.
2. Our forefathers were sincere people who led a **simple life** and held fast onto **deen**.
3. They fought against injustices they were faced with.
4. We should keep the legacy of our forefathers alive.
5. We should not become a barrier from people accepting Islam.

www.ingramcontent.com/pod-product-compliance
Lightning Source LLC
LaVergne TN
LVHW060140080526
838202LV00049B/4040